"Life's Wake-Up Calls"

Tanny McCarthy Mann

Acknowledgements

Thanks must go out to two people who encouraged me and gave their time and expertise. To my son, Brent Mann, for his perceptive comments and for reading and proofing numerous drafts of this book. Brent listened to my dream and encouraged me to do it. He was always willing to work with me on ideas and concepts.

To Dennis Coates, who worked inputting draft-after-draft of my thoughts into the computer. His patience and sense of humor saw me through this project.

With love and support from Dennis and Brent this workbook has been created and was a pleasure to write. Thanks, guys.

I must not forget Carole Flynn, who I could always count on for expert word processing. My dear friend, Karen Wilkening, who spent endless hours editing my work. Mary Molloy, my book reviewer and strategist, whose ideas were incredibly helpful. Bob Burg, who was never too busy to share knowledge on publishing and marketing. To Ellen Lynch, who always believed in me.

To all the people who, over the years, put their trust in me to help them find their way when they didn't know where to turn.

Introduction

Dear Reader,

I wrote this book for you. It may well be the most important book you've ever held in your hands. If you are not where you wish to be professionally or personally – "not to worry." They say that when you are ready, the teacher appears. I'm a lifestyle coach, who has helped thousands of people start living the life they desire and deserve.

Allow me the privilege of showing you the way to wake up and become unstuck.

The format I've used will provide you with the formula to succeed and the skills necessary to reach your goals and live a successful life. I will introduce you to thought processes and concepts that will help you become unstuck. It's time to look at your behavior, re-think things and try new approaches. This is an exciting time for you. You're designing your own future. You're formulating a plan that encompasses the "whole you," emotional – physical – mental – career – relationships – spiritual. This workbook is your personal game plan, please write in it. Adding your own notes, comments, thoughts and action plans will assure your success. Read each page and re-read any parts that are new to you so you fully understand the concepts.

What you learn in this book is powerful and personal. It will guide you to discover who you are, what you want and what it takes for you to get it.

My personal philosophy is, "If you choose to win, you will." The future is a potential; you design it. (Together we will design it.)

The fact that I was born neither brilliant, beautiful nor wealthy and have succeeded allows me to say unequivocally, "What you need to succeed you already have." As your coach I'll help you discover it.

My goal is to help you become your own coach, capable of responding successfully to the challenges and changes you're facing now and will continue to face. Life is change. It's a process not a destination.

Change requires some risk taking because it will take you out of your comfort zone. Risk taking is emotional, but not taking risks is "quiet death" – being stuck. Be assured that you can take charge of change by creating a game plan that will work for you.

So many people "sleepwalk through life." I'm here to wake you up. How have I made my own miracles happen? Looking back, I see that I refused to accept that anyone or anything could stand in the way of what I wanted in my life. I took control. I accepted responsibility for how my life looked (and I didn't like it). I understood there were some things I couldn't change; however, I could control my reactions to them. There were many things I could change, though. It was clear I was responsible for what my future would be. I figured out what a fulfilling life would look like to me and I went after it with a vengeance. This book contains everything I needed to know to make my dreams real; it can do the same for you. The information you now have at your fingertips represents thousands of hours of research on my part. In essence, I have done the homework for you.

Please keep an open mind to new thoughts, ideas, approaches – stay positive, risk, do the exercises, answer the questions, apply new insights into your life, look at your options, be creative, become a possibility thinker.

This is an interactive workbook, a powerful tool for putting a life plan into action. By adding your thoughts and highlighting things of particular importance to you, you'll make it your own. Each chapter contains stand alone sections with a review at the end. Focus on what is most relevant to where you are now. Please take the time to write in the review pages. This will help you reach your goals. It's important to know if you are winning or losing at any given moment.

Most people put more time and energy into planning their yearly vacation than in planning their life. I urge you to be the exception. I firmly believe you will reach your goals and enjoy the life you can now only dream of. If you accept the challenge.

No one can give you the life you want.
No one can take it away.
It's time to answer your Wake-Up Call.

What you can expect from this book...

The exercise on pages 7 through 9, "Taking Stock," will provide you with a base line, an idea of where you stand now with respect to certain important areas in your life. This same exercise is repeated in the book's last chapter. I guarantee that by the time you do the exercise for the second time, you'll have gained many valuable insights. After doing the exercises, answering the questions, writing your thoughts in the margins, highlighting the most important issues and writing in the review pages at the end of every chapter, you will be a changed person. You will have answered Life's Wake-Up Calls and be on the way to becoming unstuck. The process you're beginning will be intellectually stimulating and challenging and, at times, emotionally draining. If it seems overwhelming, hang in there - you're going to love the results. I wish I could promise that each new undertaking would be easy. That each risk would have a positive outcome, but that's not realistic. Everything worthwhile in life has a price tag. Life does not hand out guarantees. (If it did, I guess I was standing in the wrong line.)

By making a commitment to yourself, you will have a clear picture of who you are, what you really want and what it's going to take to start living your dreams. So, let's begin this process with enthusiasm. You are holding in your hands the foundation for creating the life you desire and deserve. Let's go!

So, pick up your pen and highlighter - I will coach you!

TABLE OF CONTENTS

CHAPTER 1: **"Life's Wake-Up Calls"**   p. 1
Are you stuck? Growing through change. Wake up your life is calling! Have you been collaborating in your own defeat? Are you a fly in a jar? Monkey traps. Understanding your frozen feelings. Destructive habits. Fence-sitters anonymous. Own your behavior. Breakthrough thinking.

CHAPTER 2: **"Insight"**   p. 49
Understanding the purpose of your life. What makes you happy. Creating a mission statement. The power of belief. Over-beliefs. Beliefs shape your life. New belief systems. Personal values. How do you measure success? For insight. What's good about my life?

CHAPTER 3: **"Personal Mastery/Taking Responsibility"**   p. 79
What am I responsible for? Procrastination. Design your future – your four futures. Creating your preferable futures. What can I live with/without? Risky business How you package "you." Personal energy. Body language. The power of good communication skills. Dealing with shyness. Eye power. Networking skills. Networking for a job.

CHAPTER 4: **"Understanding Stress"**   p. 123
Identifying stress. Making sense of life's changes. Letting go. Getting through life changes. Handling rejection. The stress of loneliness. The stress of mistakes and failure. The stress of anger. Whatever happens, there are only five things you can do. A simpler life. Life too stressed? Simplify, simplify. The seasons of your life. SAD (Seasonal Affective Disorder) adds to stress. Tanny's stress busters. Where's your sense of humor?

CHAPTER 5: **"Setting Goals"**   p. 177
Mastery of goal setting. A clear purpose. Goals or gleams? Beware of ghost goals. Goals as motivational tools. My life line. Creating the life you desire. Current reality and revising goals. Making things happen. The big picture. Your personal goal setting plan. Your planning wall. Become a goal setter. Scared Free.

CHAPTER 6: **"Tanny's Strategies for Success"** p. 227
How to get what you want! Trade-offs. Mind mapping.
Time management. Why bother to plan? How to plan.
How to do a "TO-DO" list. Practical hints for planning.

CHAPTER 7: **"Become a Problem Solver"** p. 261
Your life is a problem-solving adventure! The art of
negotiating. Creativity. Self-discipline. Commitment.
Persistence. Problem solving made easy. Turning complaints
into objectives. A theoretical problem. "Whats."

CHAPTER 8: **"The Power of Your Subconscious Mind"** p. 293
Your conscious mind. Your subconscious mind. Your
subconscious is your control system. Subconscious needs.
Mental picture power. Turn off unwanted mental pictures.
Thoughts are "Things." Creative visualization. Imagine your
future into reality. "As if."

CHAPTER 9: **"Carpe Vitam!" (Seize Life)** p. 337
Personal magic. Championship living. Tanny's suggestion
checklist. Wrap-up.

Final words from Tanny

CHAPTER 1

"Life's Wake-Up Calls"

CHAPTER 1 – TABLE OF CONTENTS

Section		Page
1	Are You Stuck?	5
	Exercise: Taking Stock	
	Exercise: MY Bio	10
2	Growing through Change	11
	Exercise: MY Contract with Myself	14
3	Wake Up – Your Life Is Calling!	15
	Exercise: Wake-Up Calls in MY Life	15
	Exercise: MY New Path	16
	Exercise: MY Associates	17
	Exercise: MY Life's Wish List	19
4	Have You Been Collaborating in Your Own Defeat?	20
	Exercise: MY Action Plan	23
5	Are You a Fly in a Jar?	24
6	Monkey Traps	25
	Exercise: MY Monkey Traps	25
7	Understanding Your Frozen Feelings	26
	Exercise: MY Frozen Feelings	27
8	Destructive Habits	28
	Exercise: Where I'm Stuck	28
	Exercise: MY Unresolved Hurts	32
9	Fence-Sitters Anonymous	33
	Exercise: MY Fence-Sitting	37

Life's Wake-Up Calls   p. 3

10	Own Your Behavior	38
	Exercise: I Created This	40
11	Breakthrough Thinking	41
	Exercise: MY Breakthroughs	43
	Exercise: MY Ideas	45

Section 1

Are You Stuck?

Over and over I hear...

> "Tanny, I feel stuck. I'm confused, immobilized, in limbo. I'm trying but I can't get started. I can't seem to keep going. I become discouraged."
>
> "What can I do? Help!"

I want you to know that there is a reason why you get "stuck," and that this book will give you the tools to

GET UNSTUCK!!

In a stuck state, you live on "automatic pilot" – your unconscious has you automatically respond in old, familiar ways, even in <u>new</u> situations. That is why

HISTORY REPEATS ITSELF!

Want new results? You won't get them from old patterns of behavior. Want to get unstuck and realize more of the great potential of your life?

START WORKING ON <u>YOURSELF</u> FIRST
– NOT YOUR CIRCUMSTANCES.

Being stuck isn't a fun place to find yourself. Beginnings are difficult because you are confronting internal psychological resistance and the realization that <u>it's tough out there</u>!

THE TOUGHEST BATTLES IN YOUR LIFE ARE FOUGHT INTERNALLY.
ALL MEANINGFUL CHANGE COMES FROM THE INSIDE!

So, has your clock stopped? Some people's clocks just plain stop. If you realize this has happened to you, it's time to "Wake up!" If you feel like a clock that has wound down, let's wind you up so you can start ticking again.

I have some wind-up clocks in my home. Some need to be wound weekly, some once a year. Just before these clocks need their "wind up" they start to slow down and lose a few minutes. I'm careful to make sure they don't stop. Let's do the same for you!

We, at times, build our own prison and become our own jailkeeper. To respond to your wake-up calls, you must let go of old traumas, old grievances, past failures, and the accumulated baggage that has long outlived its usefulness. Some people almost seem to delight in holding onto ghosts from the past. This behavior is self-destructive.

WHY ARE **WAKE-UP CALLS** GOOD FOR YOU?

Wake-Up Calls are often the catalyst for choosing your new direction – don't press the snooze button. Answer the call. It's your choice. It will only go off so many times before it's too late and then you'll really start feeling the pain you've been avoiding.

Wake-Up Calls you wish to label either positive or negative are really neutral. Start viewing **Wake-Up Calls** as your opportunity to learn to look at your life differently. Learn to look at the big picture.

> *Stay awake – **Wake-Up Calls** are the catalyst for you to choose a new direction*
>
> *Stay awake – be open to the options – new opportunities – new possibilities*
>
> *The smart thing to do is to find new behavior*
>
> *"Stuff" (old behavior, old patterns) that is no longer working for you – let go of it!*
>
> *Stop recycling your internal garbage – your past choices influence but do not control your destiny*

I will help you wake up and stay awake. Wake up your potential.

At times you can't awaken by yourself. You need to be looked after by someone who isn't asleep! This is my job – to wake you up and make sure you don't fall asleep again!

EXERCISE

Taking Stock
The way my life looks now

Date: _____
(If needed, use more paper)

You Are Here!

Taking Stock

Personally, right now I.....

_____

Career-Wise right now I.....

_____

Financially, right now I.....

_____

EXERCISE

Taking Stock
The way my life looks now

Date: _____
(If needed, use more paper)

Physically, right now I.....

_____
_____
_____
_____
_____
_____
_____

Socially, right now I.....

_____
_____
_____
_____
_____
_____
_____

Intellectually, right now I.....

_____
_____
_____
_____
_____
_____
_____

Taking Stock

EXERCISE

Taking Stock
The way my life looks now

Date: _____
(If needed, use more paper)

Emotionally, right now I.....
_____
_____
_____
_____
_____
_____
_____

Spiritually, right now I.....
_____
_____
_____
_____
_____
_____
_____

Relationships, right now I.....
_____
_____
_____
_____
_____
_____
_____
_____

Taking Stock

Life's Wake-Up Calls   p. 9

EXERCISE

Please write a brief "bio" (biography) of your life up to the present. Using an outline form instead of complete sentences, list the highlights of your life. Try to write as an objective journalist, using the third person (he/she).

MY "Bio"

Born _____ **through Today** _____

_____
_____
_____
_____
_____
_____
_____
_____
_____
_____
_____
_____
_____
_____
_____
_____
_____
_____
_____
_____
_____
_____
_____
_____
_____
_____
_____
_____
_____

Life's Wake-Up Calls   p. 10

Section 2

Growing through Change

Growing – reaching new levels of understanding, self-awareness and success – is one of the main goals of life.

GROWTH NEVER ENDS.

Even when you reach higher levels, there are still further levels to go. Without growth, there is a contraction of life-force energy. With growth, you feel vibrant, alive, healthy and joyful!

The more you want to grow with all your being, the more change you must deal with. You will want to have flexible beliefs, an open mind and trust that the universe is friendly. You can grow with joy rather than struggle.

*If you believe that growth comes from struggle,
you will create crises by which to grow!*

One of the greatest gifts you can give yourself is to dissolve any negative pictures you have about growth and change. Growth comes from living life fully and welcoming opportunities to change.

I find most people approach change from one of two directions. Which path do you normally take? (check one)

- ❏ People afraid of change remain in familiar though painful situations. They may want to change, but are too afraid to take the risk.

- ❏ People who change too quickly or too often, without the consideration and planning necessary to make change successful.

Change can only happen in the present. The present is always a chance to begin again. Sometimes it is only in retrospect that we can see that we were given another chance at life, a new relationship or job, but because we were too busy reacting to the past, we missed the opportunity at something new.

We are given plenty of opportunities, but we undermine them!

To ask for another <u>relationship</u> or <u>job</u> is not helpful if we're going to show up in the new situation exactly as we showed up in the last one!

Change is the key!

Gandhi said, "We must BE the change."

To help either type, I encourage you to make a "contract" with yourself. This contract will fulfill several purposes. First, it will give you permission to succeed and it allows the belief that a good life is naturally yours and that you are deserving of success. Love yourself enough to receive.

People who have abundance, loving relationships and happiness are not more deserving or better than you. They simply expect and allow more good things to come into their lives.

A contract with yourself also makes you accountable to the most important person in your life – yourself.

Knowing that you expect a progress report from yourself will help spur you on at times when you feel like quitting.

Become accountable to yourself. Make a contract with yourself.

Start Now to Build a Relationship with Yourself

Life's greatest battles are fought each hour, each day, in the quiet part of your heart and soul.

- Learn to win the battles there.
- Learn to settle any inward conflicts and you will start to feel more peaceful.
- Learn what you are about. Once you master inner conflicts, the outward victories will begin to flow easily.

The secret to working from the inside out is to obey and educate, listen to your conscience, learn to be honest with "who you are" and what you believe in – your value system – and live it. This requires total honesty on your part. You will have it all once you become true to yourself. Live your life with integrity centered on good principles. Be value-driven and independent.

CONTRACT (with myself)

I am making a commitment to me.

My commitment is to take total responsibility for myself.

To live the life I want, I will...

I.	Clearly understand my value system.
II.	Define what I want.
III.	Write down my goals.
IV.	Take action to achieve them.
V.	Work towards them daily to move forward.
VI.	Set deadlines.
VII.	Be open to all possibilities.
VIII.	Enjoy the process.
IX.	Review them.
X.	Acknowledge my accomplishments.
XI.	Reward myself.
XII.	Enjoy meeting the goal.
XIII.	Move on to new goals.

EXERCISE

MY Contract with Myself

Contract with myself:

Life's Wake-Up Calls   p. 14

Section 3

Wake Up – Your Life Is Calling!

Suddenly things change – voluntarily or involuntarily – and you're off balance. Can you identify with anything on the following list?

Deaths	*Job Change/Loss of Job*	*Other*
Health Change	*Spiritual Awakening*	_____
Physical Move	*New Relationship*	_____
Deep Loss	*Change in Children's Lives*	_____
Retirement	*Divorce*	_____
Financial Loss	*Bankruptcy*	_____

These events act as catalysts – they are wake-up calls. These can sometimes be very painful.

What changes have occurred which you must now take control of that were not your choice?

EXERCISE

Wake-Up Calls in MY Life

Changes I had no control over which I must deal with…

1) _____
2) _____
3) _____
4) _____
5) _____

Life's Wake-Up Calls   p. 15

Look at what's not working in your present life. Be painfully honest with this list.

EXERCISE

What positive steps can you take to help you start on a new path?

1) _____
2) _____
3) _____
4) _____
5) _____

MY New Path

When you're stuck "in a rut," and ready for a change, getting out is the fun part. Oh, there's work involved, of course – you'll be learning some new skills, doing some honest self-evaluation and performing some mental exercises that I guarantee will help you...

Associates

All our close associations influence our quality of life in ways we may never realize. I'd like to encourage you to think about the positive and negative influences of people currently in your life.

EXERCISE

Please make a list of all the people you currently associate with. They may be relatives, friends, co-workers, neighbors, people from your health club, organizations you belong to, your church or synagogue.

Then, next to each name, assign either a "+" or a "-" to indicate an overall positive or negative influence on your present life (use initials if you wish). Be objective and honest.

MY Associates

Name (or initials)	+ or -	Name (or initials)	+ or -

While you may not have total control regarding how much time you must spend with a relative or co-worker assigned a "–", you can choose to spend more time with associates you know have a positive, upbeat, supportive influence on your life! Don't hang out with an easy crowd. Seek out people who challenge you - be around people who expect a lot of themselves and who stimulate and bring out the best in you.

When you're stuck, your morale is lower than usual. It's a time when you need encouragement and permission to succeed. As you embark on a mission to unstick what's <u>not working</u> in your life, seek encouraging, positive associates. I want you to be more aware of the effect of your current daily associations.

Time for another exercise. Right now I'm only going to ask you to sit back, relax, and think, meditate and daydream about everything important that you've ever wanted <u>to do, to have and to be</u>. Go back to your childhood and write down the urges and desires you've had for your life. Don't hesitate to include things you've never had a chance to explore realistically. *This is your life's wish list!*

Now, pick up your pen again and make at least <u>least</u> 20 entries on the next page.

IT'S YOUR TURN
exercise on next page

Life's Wake-Up Calls   p. 18

EXERCISE

Everything important I've ever wanted to Do, to Have and to Be

MY Life's Wish List

Priority No.	Describe Briefly

When you have 20 entries, assign priority numbers to each, starting with the number "1". This exercise is for insight into your unfulfilled dreams.

Of course, having insight is great. However, ultimately, you must do something different or you will remain stuck!

Section 3

Have You Been Collaborating in Your Own Defeat?

Life is an endless unfolding – a process of self-discovery.

There's something you may not know about yourself. You have within you more resources and energy than have ever been tapped. Talents that have never been exploited – more strengths than have been tested. More to give than you have ever given. You're aware of some of the gifts that you have left underdeveloped. I'm telling you that you have gifts and possibilities you don't even know about.

This book will help you identify them.

Self-preoccupation is a prison. Commitments beyond the self can get you out of prison. The future is shaped by people who *believe* in the future. People of vision and vitality have always been prepared to shape their future in ventures of unknown outcome. If everyone always looked before they leaped, we would still be living in caves.

Life is tumultuous – an endless losing and regaining of balance, a continuous struggle – never an assured victory. Nothing is ever finally safe. Every important battle is fought and refought.

The door to opportunity doesn't close as long as you are reasonably healthy. There are always opportunities to grow and enrich your life.

Meaning is something you must build into your life. It is not something you stumble across. You build it out of your past – out of your loyalties and affections – out of your experiences, out of your own unique talents and understandings, out of the things you believe in, out of the people and things that you love, out of the values for which you stand and have sacrificed for. I'm sure you have heard people say, "My life has no meaning." Or, maybe *you* have uttered these words? Let's see where you are and look at some options to put "meaning" back into your life.

Life's Wake-Up Calls   p. 20

You must understand...

> YOU CANNOT EXPECT DIFFERENT RESULTS FROM THE SAME OLD BEHAVIOR. IF THE BEHAVIOR YOU'RE USING IS NOT GETTING YOU THE RESULTS YOU WISH, IT'S TIME TO CHANGE YOUR BEHAVIOR.

Knowing who you are and what makes you tick is rewarding but is of little value in a practical sense if you don't use the knowledge to meet your goals.

The cure for getting unstuck is – *Taking Action*.

Action is the antidote for learned helplessness. Becoming active reduces anxiety and stress. Once you get going – *Keep Going*.

When I was in high school my Grandfather gave me his old Studebaker to drive. Did you ever have a car with a clutch that needed a push? Remember how people would get behind and push? Once it started, it puttered a bit, threatening to stall. You had to concentrate and know how to work the clutch, letting it out e-a-s-y. You didn't want to lose it. Once the momentum built up, OFF YOU WENT. You were AFRAID to stop too soon (until the engine warmed up), only to have to go through the same process. Once you started going at a good clip, you were all set!

It's the same with you – keep the momentum going once you start. People who give you the push will yell encouragement to you...

> KEEP GOING! KEEP GOING!

This is what I want you to do! Get going and keep going. I'll give you the push; however, it's up to you to keep going. Sure there will be setbacks and some failure. You've heard of MURPHY'S LAW:

> IF SOMETHING CAN GO WRONG, IT WILL!

When obstacles, challenges or mistakes occur, I will be encouraging you to

> HANG IN THERE!

You must keep going forward. Please realize that personal growth/progress does not move along in a set pattern. You will hit plateaus, progress at times in baby steps. Change is gradual; sometimes we go two steps ahead, one back. New obstacles come into play. Don't become discouraged. At times, you'll feel as if you're back at square one. Although it may seem like square one, I can assure you that you are moving ahead.

I'd like you to ask yourself – **why do I get up in the morning?**

The reasons sometimes become a blur.

If you're feeling like a passenger on a bus who doesn't know where the bus is going, who is surprised at where it takes you and where it stops, but you stay on for the ride, you're in for trouble. It's time for you to get off.

Change direction and know your destination. You must prepare for unexpected stops and detours and be open to unexpected options. There are many ways to reach your destination.

You're not stuck on this bus. Pull the cord – the bus will stop.

Look at where you are. This is where you allowed yourself to be. You may wish to change the direction you have been going in. Think about the destination you wish to reach. Maybe the bus ride you've been on will get you there. If this is the case, you can get back on the same bus. Be sure this is the case and not just the fact that you are comfortable and willing to accept whatever destination the bus reaches regardless of the cost to you.

Know and explore all the options available to reach your destination. There are many ways to reach your destination. Whatever mode you choose, there will be unexpected stops – possible detours, some delays, smooth sailing and some conditions you can't control. This is part of the journey. It's your decision as to how you're going to get there – whether you enjoy the journey or not is up to you.

EXERCISE

MY Action Plan

What could I do — what would I enjoy doing — to put more meaning into my life?

Section 4

Are You a Fly in a Jar?

I would like you to do a little experiment to make a very strong point about behavior that may be costing you too much!

Take a glass jar, punch holes in the lid. Put some flies in the jar. Put the cover back on. The flies will buzz around frantically trying to get out of the cramped space. Keep the lid on for a period of time and then <u>remove the cover</u>.

Guess what happens? The flies don't escape. With the lid off and the opening clear, the flies are so used to circling in the cramped jar, they continue to do so. Just when they get close to the opening, they go right back to flying in the same pattern that keeps them imprisoned.

<u>Stop acting like a fly</u>. Unfortunately, most people have the same problem – a way out of a situation is presented to us, and we ignore it and keep flying in the same imprisoning patterns.

Most people carry around so much emotional baggage from long ago that their lives feel burdensome, and they fall into painful ruts. We must try to learn and grow from setbacks and stop re-enacting similar traumas over and over. Understand, please...whatever is unresolved from the past will keep coming up over and over and be disruptive to your present and your future. Your job is to find out what unfinished business from long ago is keeping you stuck.

Life's Wake-Up Calls   p. 24

Section 6

Monkey Traps

Do you know what "Monkey Traps" are?

These are things that you won't let go of that are hurting you. The expression comes from the traps hunters use to capture baby monkeys in the wild. The trap has a piece of fruit in it. The monkey puts his hand into the trap to get the fruit. If the monkey would <u>let go</u> of the fruit, he could easily pull his hand out. However, he will not <u>let go</u> of the fruit – the hunter catches him unharmed.

Examples of Monkey Traps for humans are:

1. Thinking you don't deserve good things to happen to you
2. Believing all people are not trustworthy
3. Thinking things can only be done one way (refusing to look at options)
4. The need to always be right
5. I'm too old
6. I'm not smart enough
7. I don't know the right people

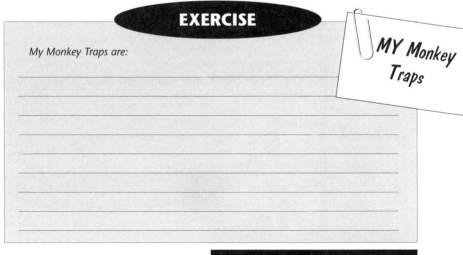

EXERCISE

My Monkey Traps are:

MY Monkey Traps

Life's Wake-Up Calls

Section 7

Understanding Your Frozen Feelings

Let's think of your feelings as wrapped packages that you keep in an enormous freezer in your basement. You've been putting packages into your freezer for years, but seldom taken anything out. The freezer is loaded with these wrapped packages (your emotions), all of which were labeled at one time. Age has worn off some of the labels. The "stuff" you've put in years ago is deep inside, and you have forgotten what it is and just how it got there. On occasion, someone opens the freezer to find something and does not close the lid. Some of the packages tumble out and become partially unthawed, but you come along and stick these packages back into your freezer.

Before the power goes off and <u>the whole mess thaws out</u>, let's take out one package at a time – <u>thaw it out</u> – <u>look at it</u> – accept it as something we own, and then dispose of it.

As a child, you learned how to hide your feelings; many of your feelings were not acceptable to the adults around you. These suppressed feelings are extremely harmful. Anger, guilt, regret, etc. cause an enormous amount of stress on your body – and may cause physical illness. What you can't afford to have happen is to find yourself in a depression, a total freezing of who you are.

It's vital you get in touch with your feelings – and work through any childhood issues by talking about them and expressing them in acceptable ways – and letting go.

It's risky business to get in touch with your feelings; however, to grow, become all you were meant to be, you must learn to participate in life and interact with people. A healthy approach for you is to be totally honest with yourself and those who are important to you on how you feel about issues as they occur. Keep current with your feelings. This will keep you from stuffing more into your freezer, only to have to deal with it at a later date. We never know when we may "lose power," which would result in having to deal with a "frozen issue" at an inconvenient or inappropriate time in the future. Why risk it? It's time to thaw your frozen (unresolved) issues.

I do not want to minimize the importance of this serious subject. Some issues you can deal with on your own. Some situations and people would benefit by professional help from a qualified psychologist or psychiatrist.

EXERCISE

MY Frozen Feelings

List five frozen feelings:

1) _____
2) _____
3) _____
4) _____
5) _____

Are these issues I can deal with, or would I be wise to seek professional help?

Section 8

Destructive Habits

We as humans carry around so much emotional baggage from our past that our lives feel like a burden. We get "stuck" – instead of learning and growing from our frustrations, most of us have the habit of re-enacting similar traumas over and over again. Please "wake up" to the fact that unresolved situations from the past will find a way to disrupt your life now and in the future. For a new beginning you need to uncover what "unfinished business" is keeping you stuck.

For a truly new beginning, you must break free of any painful ruts and find a way for the new you to reach your goals.

Where am I stuck? Let's pretend for a moment...

EXERCISE

Where I'm Stuck

A. *If you could improve one thing about your primary relationship (or lack of one), what would it be?*

What would you do about it?

Life's Wake-Up Calls   p. 28

B. *If you could change one thing about your work life (or daily activities at home), what would you change?*

_____

_____

What would you do about it?

_____

_____

_____

_____

C. *If you could clear up one problem with a family member, what and with whom would it be?*

_____

_____

What would you do about it?

_____

_____

_____

_____

D. *If you could heal any unresolved hurt from the past, what would it be?*

_____

_____

What would you do about it?

_____

_____

_____

_____

I'm sure there are some areas in your life that you wish were different. Please understand that in order for you to make real progress in any area of your life, there's something you must know: The method you choose will be the factor that will get you on the right path or will find you making the same mistakes over and over.

There are choices when you wish to improve any important situation in your life.

Most people plunge ahead without stopping to resolve the "emotional baggage" they have inside concerning the issue. This is definitely asking for trouble. Sooner or later the unresolved stuff will come back to haunt you. It's a mistake to ignore or deny unfinished business in any area of your life. In personal relationships, this is common. A new person unknowingly says or does something that reminds your subconscious of something painful in your past. You become upset with this new person when in reality the feelings you're experiencing have more to do with someone from your past. This person asks, "What did I do?…say?" Having no clue that she opened (unintentionally) frozen feelings from your past. What happens is you will often take out on this new person the unfinished business you have with the person in your past.

There is a solution to this serious matter. You have heard it before: "Let go." Letting go will allow you to be successful in new relationships. What you need to remember is that whenever you get upset with someone it's usually because they have (unintentionally) re-triggered an unresolved hurt from your past. STOP – think before you start attacking the new person. Take a moment (physically excuse yourself) and ask yourself, "What's really going on here? What frozen feelings from the past are being triggered? What's causing me to feel so angry, sad, disappointed or upset right now?" Take the time to write them down and really examine them.

Letting go will improve the way you handle difficult situations and people.

Suggestions:

Next time your buttons get pushed – in a personal relationship, work environment or any situation – STOP – unwind – communicate. Ask what past hurts and bad experiences are making you so emotional.

In relationships you choose to keep, relationships that are important to you, I suggest you make the investment. You will start to build healthy ways of relating.

Most people deny they have unresolved hurts from prior experiences. Most people deny that the past has anything to do with their current problems. This is not so. This is "inner hard work." Most people avoid hard work, but you don't or you would not be reading this.

The key to solving current problems is to understand how they are created by unresolved issues from the past.

This is a powerful skill I highly suggest you master. Stop paying the high price of this habit of ignoring or denying your hurts from the past. You have the ability to sort out your inner feelings each time you sense a new situation is being affected by issues from your past. Unfortunately, this is a skill not taught in school or at home. If you are tired of making the same mistakes over and over in relationships, what have you got to lose in trying this method of looking at situations? You will no longer be a victim of your past. "Your past" does not equal "your future." Use your past as a learning experience.

Allow the tough stuff you've been through to be of value to you by understanding it.

Let go.

Reminders:

1. Be aware – every time you experience some deep emotion it has something to do with the present, but more importantly with unfinished business.
2. Hidden beliefs we carry as a result of previous hurts are often irrational.
3. Releasing is important – unresolved frozen feelings lodge in your body. These are potentially dangerous to your physical and mental health and must be released. Please find a safe way to do this.
4. Start putting into practice the lessons and strengths you now have. Give yourself a fresh start. Practice clear communications. Become skillful at resolving conflicts – don't let things go into crisis before you act – don't be afraid to negotiate for your needs.

EXERCISE

Ask yourself — what unfinished business do I carry into each new reltionship? Personally? Career? Etc.?

MY Unresolved Hurts

Section 9

Fence-Sitters Anonymous

"Stopping Your Creative Mind – It's Costing You."

What incredible excuses do you come up with? What amazing interruptions, diversions do you create? Getting sick? Too busy? What uncanny talents do you possess to procrastinate?

Sitting on the fence? Unable to make a decision or follow through with commitments? Do you hear yourself saying, "I can't decide...maybe I should wait until I feel more certain." Learn to take the next step! You have good intentions to take the necessary step to move forward in the area in which you feel stuck. <u>However,</u> good intentions are not enough. Just when you must make the commitment, and get moving, something happens that causes you to stop or stall. Why? What causes people to stall, stop, feel caught and end up sitting on the fence? What makes people become distracted so easily?

Everyone has moments of indecision, or hesitation, when moving forward. However, with some people, it is a chronic and costly way of life. This behavior of stalling and stopping limits the goals you will reach in your life and diminishes your self-respect. You begin to feel bad about yourself because of the many promises you made to yourself but never kept. You stand to lose what you want (opportunities, friendships, relationships, etc.) because you didn't make your mind up until it was too late. Regret and resentment for what could have been are emotions you'll have to deal with.

"I SHOULD HAVE" – If this is something you have heard yourself say over the years, it's time to look at some new behavior for yourself.

Why do you sit on the fence?

The #1 reason people procrastinate is that they learned it is safer to stall than to risk.

> *At times, you might have gotten attention for not making a decision.*
>
> *At times, you may have received help and assistance from others that you would not have received if you had made up your mind.*
>
> *At times, you don't want to deal with criticism, failure, disapproval.*
>
> *At times, you avoided leaving an uncomfortable (but familiar) situation because you were not sure you could replace it with something better.*
>
> *At times, you stall finishing something you aren't sure you can do well, so people can't find fault with it.*

People who can't make decisions don't trust themselves, so others lose trust and confidence in them. If you're anxious about making decisions, you probably learned indecisiveness as a young child.

Being indecisive can cost you. People will take advantage of your procrastination and make decisions for you that will be in their best interest, not yours.

Procrastination is a difficult habit to change. You must understand why you do it and work through the emotional reasons you are a "fence-sitter." The next step is to take chances.

> *It's risky business to move out of the known to the unknown.*
>
> *Your emotional baggage and fears of the past keep you on the fence.*
>
> *You will find excuses for not following through until you come to terms with it.*

Your mind is saying, "It's not safe" to step out, and it will help you create ways of stalling.

When your mind is filled with doubt, you have options:

1. You can go into your normal mode of procrastination.

2. You can take a look at what's going on with your emotions and move forward.

3. You can stop letting your fears ruin your plans and ask yourself:

    – What issues need to be resolved so I can move forward?

    – Why am I hesitating?

    – What am I afraid of?

    – Is this fear related to a past bad experience?

    – What can I do to turn this fear into valuable clues of what I don't want to have happen again?

    – What can I do to make this time better than past experiences?

    – What have I learned to help me manage this situation with more clarity, openness and creativity?

Try not to be shut down by your fears, try to progress forward even when you feel anxious, insecure. Don't ignore insecurities – use them to help you have new insight to move forward.

When you're in a rut – STOP – and remind yourself that you have been in ruts before and have succeeded.

This is not always easy work – to break through a pattern of putting off making decisions, you may have to give up some of your oldest habits and beliefs. <u>NOT AN EASY TASK</u>.

Take time to look at areas in your life in which you are sitting on the fence:
1. Think – what's holding me back?
2. Think – what do I need to do to resolve it?
3. What self-limiting attitude/habit/belief should I look at?

Face the fact that as a procrastinator you have become extremely talented at coming up with ways to stall and put off following through on a decision. You need to have a plan, an equally creative way to overcome this.

You need tools to stop you from your usual stalling and to help you get moving when indecision starts to step in.

Suggestion: When faced with a situation, let yourself have just <u>two</u> options. Eliminate weaker ones – <u>focus on two</u>. Write them down.

Option 1 _____

Option 2 _____

That's all you're allowed. No more, "On the other hand…"

Suggestion: Make an honest assessment of what you're losing, whom you're neglecting, and what you're missing out on by sitting on the fence. Ask yourself if this indecision distracts you from other goals and responsibilities? Is this indecision hurting or upsetting people you love? Is this behavior costing you in terms of trust others have in you or the trust you have in yourself?

This is an overview of the "hidden costs" so you can look at any situation you're stalling on in an honest manner.

The questions are:

The costs to me physically – emotionally – interpersonally – financially – socially.

Ask yourself, is the cost too high?

EXERCISE

MY Fence-Sitting

What have I been sitting on the fence about?

What do I plan to do about it?

Section 10

Own Your Behavior

Until you stop looking at a situation and saying, "I didn't create this," you're letting the situation remain beyond your control. You're saying there's nothing you can do about this, that it must remain this way forever. As soon as you say, "I created this," you make it your own. You accept responsibility for it. When you accept responsibility for creating it, you're then ready to assume responsibility for changing it. You take control of your life. I feel this is vital for you to understand. You can't control the universe. *However, you can control your reactions to life's sometimes unpleasant and painful events.* Things which you cannot control you must still accept as fact. This is where life has placed you.

> STOP PUTTING YOUR WANTS, NEEDS AND DESIRES ON THE BACK BURNER.

Most people put more time, thought and energy into planning a trip than they do into their life plan. Would you start on a trip without a destination, a map? I doubt if you would end up where you wanted to be without preparation. Many people just let life happen.

> AREN'T YOU WORTH MORE THAN THAT?

For your dreams to come true, you must ...

> *Accept responsibility* for having created things the way they are in your life right now. How your life looks right now is how you have set it up.
>
> *Understand it's totally up to you* to change what you wish to change. Stop the blame game.
>
> *Take control of your life.* This happens in your mind, it's a mind set. When you don't take control, you hand the power over to someone else.

As you read this book and do the exercises, remember that there is no physical action, besides writing, involved in what I'm asking you to do.

Essentially, all I am asking that you do is make a positive shift in your attitude. A positive attitude constitutes the vital, crucial beginning of an entirely new approach to life. A new approach that means you are the cause of what happens to you from now on.

THIS IS GOOD NEWS.

Learn to be your own best friend.

Remember: You are the only one you will be spending the rest of your life with. You are loyal to your best friend, dependable, trustworthy, and keep your promise to do things for him/her, and you follow through. Do the same for yourself; learn to value yourself. Become your own biggest fan. Be as committed to yourself as you are to your best friend. Learn to like yourself as much as you like your best friend. No matter how long you've been stuck, you can start right now to change what you want to change. The day you stop blaming others for your life and know you are responsible for where you are is the day you are grown up. For some, this happens at age 7. For some, it's age 40! For some, it, regretfully, never happens. So take control and stop blaming others for where you are in your life.

A great start is that you are holding this book in your hands!

When you are stuck, there is no motion. It's at these times you need a script to follow which feeds you your lines and has the stage set for you. At these times in your life, you desperately need structure. The MORE you feel stuck, the more structure you need at the moment. The structure will give you a feeling of control, it will put you in balance and relieve the worry and anxiety.

You need a plan...that's what you're doing now. You should feel good about this.

EXERCISE

I Created This

What have I refused to own until now?

Now that I accept responsibility for it, I plan to change, stop blaming and take control by doing...

Section 11

Breakthrough Thinking

It's time for breakthrough thinking to become a part fo your life. Start to see things in a different light. You're open to new possibilities, to new begginnings. Breakthrough thinking results from a raw moment when you "let go of your usual assumptions." The destructive thought processess that have kept you from moving forward until now. You see something different – a possibility – a new beginning – you have the urge to create, a light-bulb turns on in your brain!

This is an exciting time for you. You don't have the answers as to how you will achieve what you wish. You will make it up as you go along, which is a creative approach to solving your situation. You do not have any guarantees that it will work. However, you're willing to risk.

To get from here

To here where you wish to be

(your stuck position)　　　**YOU MUST LET GO**　　　(unstuck)

You are hanging out in the void.

This will be a very exciting time, a creative time and there will be risk involved.

Life's Wake-Up Calls · p. 41

**LEAVING THE KNOWN (that is no longer working for you)
CREATING SOMETHING NEW**

CREATING YOUR FUTURE THE WAY YOU WANT IT TO LOOK

You understand that

"The future is a potential – you design it"

The future is not "out there" waiting to happen to you. You can design it – conjure it up to make it look the way you want it to look!

Become aware of **"Breakthrough Thinking."** Life's **Wake-Up Calls** are the catalysts to propel you forward to new behavior – a risk taking – "going for it" mode. You will then let go of old anchors (monkey traps) that have held you back. If your life isn't working, let go of your comfortable cherished beliefs. Crisis in a person's life often gives one the necessary courage to try something new. You have the choice to look at a crisis as a setback or as an opportunity. One door shuts, another one opens (if you allow it). You may become frustrated or fascinated with life. Choose to become fascinated with events that come into your life. It's healthy and more fun and profitable. "Should have" and "could have" are sad words. Start today to make your dreams a reality. Don't live in the past.

Yesterday is dead and gone. No matter how hard you try, you can't get it back. Where you are right now is where you have put yourself. Accept it. You're responsible for your future.

The future is a potential. You are in control. The choices and challenges are

IT'S YOUR TURN
exercise on next page

EXERCISE

MY Breakthroughs

Where would you like to make a breakthrough in your life?

Physically

Emotionally

Spiritually

Socially

Relationship

Financially

Other

Life's Wake-Up Calls   p. 43

The power of **"A Single Idea."**

A Single Idea can change your life .
Put that one good idea to work in your life.

Look and listen for the Aha! A Flash!

It's a moment of clarity when you intuitively know this is what is right for you – you have no hesitation – all other bets are off – you know it's right – this is a breakthrough – you feel energized – powerful – positive – and are looking forward to starting whatever it is you've hit upon.

It's a time of great insight on your part. You're in control. Everything feels right. You will also feel a great amount of relief. You're on the right track. Maybe a little scared but exhilarated.

I have a question for you. Suppose you were your own therapist. What would you suggest that "you" pursue? What are the special talents, strengths, successes and passions that you have not acknowledged?

Many times, the interesting and important work you do in life is not what you intended or what your background prepared you to do.

What is it you would really like to do?

This is your life. This is not a dress rehearsal!

What idea have you had, off and on, during your life that you keep pushing down? Maybe it's time to act on it?

EXERCISE

My ideas

MY Ideas

Life's Wake-Up Calls   p. 45

Chapter 1 Review Page - Life's Wake-Up Calls

Life's Wake-Up Calls   p. 46

Life's Wake-Up Calls   p. 47

CHAPTER 2

"Insight"

CHAPTER 2 – TABLE OF CONTENTS

Section		Page
1	Understanding the Purpose of Your Life	52
	Exercise: Why Do I Get Up in the Morning?	53
2	What Makes You Happy	54
	Exercise: MY Plan to Be Happy	55
3	Creating a Mission Statement	56
	Exercise: MY Life Purpose	57
	Exercise: MY Mission Statement	61
4	The Power of Belief	62
5	Over-Beliefs	63
	Exercise: MY Over-Beliefs	64
6	Beliefs Shape Your Life	65
	Exercise: MY Positive Beliefs	66
	Exercise: MY Negative Beliefs	66
7	New Belief Systems	67
8	Personal Values	68
	Exercise: Checklist of MY Personal Values	68
9	How Do You Measure Success?	70
	Exercise: What Success Means to ME	71
	Exercise: If I Followed MY Heart	72
10	For Insight	73
	Exercise: Spend a Day Completely Alone	73
	Exercise: Spend a Day with a Child	74
	Exercise: Spend a Day with a Senior	74
11	What's Good About MY Life?	75
	Exercise: 10 Things I'm Grateful For	75

Insight p. 51

Section 1

Understanding the Purpose of Your Life

Your Philosophy – The Belief System You Live By

> Purpose is the meaning of your life
> > It is the meaning you give to your life
> > > Your Purpose is what you stand for

Purpose is greater than your goal. It's the destination of your life.

Your "Purpose" is just another way to say who you are:

> By setting goals, you discover or find your purpose.
> Your purpose gives your actions and goals a sense of meaning.

Your purpose has always been there, perhaps "hidden" under life's circumstances.

This is *very* important for you to understand, think about, and put down in black and white. Put some thought into this – take your time and answer the questions on the next page.

IT'S YOUR TURN
exercise on next page

Insight   p. 52

EXERCISE

Why Do I Get Up in the Morning?

My philosophy in life is:

_____
_____
_____
_____
_____
_____
_____
_____

This is who I am:

_____
_____
_____
_____
_____
_____
_____
_____

This is what I stand for:

_____
_____
_____
_____
_____
_____
_____
_____
_____
_____
_____
_____
_____

Insight   p. 53

Section 2

What Makes You Happy?

One of the most common causes of unhappiness is that people are attempting to live their lives on the deferred payment plan. They do not live, nor enjoy life now, but wait for some future event or occurrence. Happiness is a mental attitude. If it is not learned and practiced in the *present*, it is never experienced. If you are happy at all, you must be happy period! Not happy "because of."

Suggestion: Look at the moments of happiness or unhappiness and find out which of your opinions about the circumstances of life "made" you happy or unhappy.

Remember things that once "made" you happy but now don't make you happy any more? Why? You changed your opinion.

You are the only one who can create happiness.

One of your most important assets is to be able to create happiness.
Are you happy now?

> Now is the time to be happy.
>
> > Now is all you have.
>
> > > You can't *force* happiness into your life, but you can help it come into being by engaging in satisfying work and making a difference in other people's lives.
>
> > That is how happiness comes into being.
>
> > Tiny moments of happiness can transform your whole day.

Insight p. 54

Understand:

You are the source of your happiness.
You create your own happiness.
You are happy whenever you allow yourself to be happy.

EXERCISE

Finish this sentence: I'M VERY HAPPY WHEN I'M...

MY Plan to Be Happy

Insight p. 55

Section 3

Creating a Mission Statement

Are you clear about what you are here to do? And are you doing it?

Or are you one of the many people who have spent your entire life – <u>UNTIL NOW</u> – feeling restless, confused and unfulfilled?

Discovering your life purpose is one of the most important discoveries you will make in your lifetime. It will make such a difference that it will seem like a heavy curtain has been lifted.

Each of us has a specific purpose. It is a calling, a <u>mission,</u> or an overall theme for your life which transcends your daily activities.

If you have not experienced the level of success that you know you are capable of, or if you have felt as if something is "missing" from your life, if you are "*stuck,*" take note of this important principle:

> You will experience success in your life to the extent that you are clear about your life purpose.

Shortly, I will guide you to create your personal Mission Statement. First, you must consider what having and following a life purpose means

Many people have the misconception that following their life purpose means dedicating their life to a cause, renouncing enjoyment. *NOT SO!* Life purpose need not involve deprivation or require any undesired activities. Just the opposite: Life purpose is fun and exciting. Clues to discovering your purpose are the things that "turn you on" and get you excited.

On the following pages are issues I want you to think about. Please take your time.

Insight   p. 56

EXERCISE

MY Life Purpose

CLUES TO YOUR LIFE PURPOSE:

1. What do you love to do?
When you have spare time, how do you spend it? What do you enjoy when there are no demands on you? What would you do even if you were not paid to do it?

_____
_____
_____
_____

2. What parts of your present life activities or job do you enjoy?
It might be a small thing or task that gives you a moment of satisfaction or something to look forward to. It may be a portion of your job responsibilities.

_____
_____
_____
_____

3. What do you do well naturally?
You have some natural abilities, things that come easily. Perhaps you are naturally athletic or have a beautiful speaking voice or are a born organizer. The areas in which you naturally excel are indicators of your life purpose, particularly if YOU ENJOY THEM!

_____
_____
_____
_____

YOUR ENJOYMENT LEVEL IS THE MOST IMPORTANT GUIDE TO YOUR LIFE PURPOSE!

Insight   p. 57

4. In your own eyes, what are your ten greatest successes to date?
Put aside what others might judge and go on your gut satisfaction about something as simple as helping someone in need. Don't just list the success, also explain what it was about the accomplishment or even what makes you label it a success.

5. Is there a cause or issue about which you feel passionate?
The essence of your life purpose can be revealed through that which attracts your commitment at a deep level.

6. Has a recurring issue or problem become a lesson in your life?
If there has been a theme in your life, how would you describe it? Recurring issues often represent the key qualities you are here to develop.

Insight   p. 58

7. What do you find yourself repeatedly daydreaming about?
As covered in Chapter 8, "The Power of Your Subconscious Mind," it is in your subconscious that your beliefs reside, as well as your deepest desires. If there are images or ideas about which you repeatedly daydream (or dream during sleep), they may be aspects of your life purpose.

_____

_____

_____

_____

_____

8. What things do you want to be remembered for at the end of your life?
Let's take time right now to write your epitaph. What things will your life be incomplete without? This exercise is a good way to assess the essence of your life and goals.

My Epitaph
Write your epitaph as you would like it to be:

_____

_____

_____

_____

_____

Insight   p. 59

Now that you know that life purpose is an overall theme or mission that is unique to you, you should create a mission statement to help implement it in your life on a daily basis.

My Mission Statement
(the criteria by which I measure everything in my life)

Review it often; understand it changes as you grow, as your perspectives and values change.

> Is it based on what I currently believe in?
> Does it represent the best I have to offer?
> Does it give me a purpose and a direction?
> Do I have a strategy to help me accomplish my goal?
> Do I have the skills needed?
> What do I need to do now to be where I wish to be tomorrow?

IT'S YOUR TURN
exercise on next page

Insight   p. 60

To help you create your own mission statement, remember your mission in life is who you are, what you stand for and how you plan to spend your life.

EXERCISE

MY Mission Statement

10. The Mission Statement for My Life:

Insight p. 61

Section 4

The Power of Belief

The most powerful forces of NATURE are INVISIBLE
Heat, Sound, Wind, Gravity
The most powerful forces of MAN are INVISIBLE
Love, Desire, Thought, Belief

You can achieve whatever you believe you can...

You are the result of your beliefs...

Belief creates the actual fact.

Splendid things can be achieved once you believe that something inside of you is superior to the circumstances you are in presently.

What do you dare to believe?

Make no little plans. You can never be bigger than your plans. Place no limits, no restrictions on your goals in life.

Your plans – your goals – will shape your life.

The size of your plan will determine your future.

And, speaking of the size of your beliefs...

Insight   p. 62

Section 5

Over-Beliefs

William James professed the psychological power of over-belief, which means intensely believing that you will accomplish much more than your present conditions justify. This psychological mind set is very important to overcoming limitations (limitations that you have consciously or subconsciously placed on yourself). William James was educated at Harvard and later served as a Professor there. Much of my information in this book, dealing with psychology and philosphy, is based on his works. He was born in 1842 and died in 1910. I find his philosphy and work in psychology useful in today's world. I refer to him in this book. If the subject intrigues you, get his books from the library, there are more than 30 in print.

To help you over-believe remember:

> *You cannot judge your future by your past or present.*

Since you cannot judge your future by your present, there is absolutely no reason why you should not over-believe that you can accomplish much more than you now under-believe you can.

You should over-believe that you will be much more successful in achieving your goals, so that your life-goal becomes bigger and more worthy.

The technique of **over-belief** is to GO FOR IT – Do not just over-believe a little. Over-believe to the furthest limit of your imagination. You will be amazed to see your **over-belief** change from an impossible dream to a realizable future.

Insight   p. 63

EXERCISE

What areas would benefit from over-beliefs?

MY Over-Beliefs

Insight p. 64

Section 6

Beliefs Shape Your Life

You Create Your Own Reality – Your Own Experiences

(If you think this is not true, you probably allow someone else to create them for you!)

Your Life, the way it is today, has been created by <u>you</u>...

"What you believe of yourself comes true." This is called "self-fulfilling prophecy," and we will explore more about this power in a later chapter.

If you want to change your life, you need to change your belief systems first. Belief systems are formed from conclusions about what happened in your past.

There are different levels of belief systems...some of limited effect, others define the base of your existence.

Belief systems are like guideposts on your path.

Positive Belief Systems guide you to success and happiness.

>They are filled with power and possibilities.
>They are harmonious – for the good of people.
>
>*Examples:* I know I'm in control of my thoughts and feelings.
>I believe true friends are there when you need them.

Negative Belief Systems lead to destruction.

>They are filled with shrinking powers and possibilities and are unharmonious - violating others' rights.
>
>Examples: I can't control my future.
>Most people are ignorant and don't deserve love.

Insight   p. 65

EXERCISE

MY Positive Beliefs

My positive beliefs are:
_____
_____
_____
_____
_____
_____
_____
_____
_____
_____

EXERCISE

MY Negative Beliefs

My negative beliefs are:
_____
_____
_____
_____
_____
_____
_____
_____
_____
_____

Insight   p. 66

Section 7

New Belief Systems

In order to adopt any new belief system, you must be clear of your present belief systems. This is not an easy task – old beliefs are connected to energy that is holding the beliefs in place. This is emotional energy that is...

POSITIVE (energy): pleasure, joy – all positive emotions

or

NEGATIVE (energy): fear, pain, anger – all negative emotions

Most pain experienced in life is not real but imagined. To change, open yourself up to new experiences. You'll find your experiences today will be different from the negative experiences of the past.

You need new experiences to start building new belief systems.

You have the power to change any belief if you are willing to accept a positive belief as a new reality.

You can build a new belief system by yourself without outside influence.

It's learning to see your life from a different angle

Self-talk (positive): Self-talk is a start...

Then...start practicing whatever it is you wish to change.

Make an effort to find opportunities to practice.

Insight p. 67

Section 8

Personal Values

Values are deeply held views of what we find worthwhile. They come from parents, religion, school, culture. Some go back to childhood; others we take on as adults.

You should be aware of the temptation to let your values slip – values you say you believe in, values you act upon, which actually guide your behavior. To help you reach a better understanding of your most significant values, do the following exercise.

EXERCISE

Checklist of MY Personal Values

1. *Check the 12 values most important to you – as guides for how to behave or as components of a valued way of life. Add any of your own.*

- ❏ Achievement
- ❏ Adventure
- ❏ Affection
- ❏ Arts
- ❏ Challenging Problems
- ❏ Change
- ❏ Close Relationships
- ❏ Community
- ❏ Competition
- ❏ Cooperation
- ❏ Country
- ❏ Creativity
- ❏ Ecological Awareness
- ❏ Efficiency
- ❏ Excitement
- ❏ Fame
- ❏ Fortune
- ❏ Freedom
- ❏ Friendships
- ❏ Having a Family
- ❏ Helping Other People
- ❏ Honesty
- ❏ Independence
- ❏ Inner Harmony
- ❏ Integrity
- ❏ Job Tranquility
- ❏ Knowledge
- ❏ Location
- ❏ Loyalty
- ❏ Meaningful Work
- ❏ Money
- ❏ Nature
- ❏ Personal Development
- ❏ Physical Challenges
- ❏ Power/Authority
- ❏ Privacy
- ❏ Quality Relationships
- ❏ Recognition (others' respect)
- ❏ Security
- ❏ Self-respect
- ❏ Serenity
- ❏ Sophistication
- ❏ Stability
- ❏ Status
- ❏ Time Freedom
- ❏ Truth
- ❏ Wealth
- ❏ Wisdom
- ❏ Work with Others
- ❏ Work Alone
- ❏ _____
- ❏ _____
- ❏ _____

Insight p. 68

2. Elimination. Give up 6 of the 12 values you checked off – cross them off. Cross off one more. Now another. My 3 top values are:

1. _____ 2. _____ 3. _____

Now cross off 2 of your values – Which is the one value you care most about?

   1. _____

3. Look at the three top values on your list:

A. What do they mean?

_____
_____
_____
_____

B. How would your life be different if you practiced them?

_____
_____
_____
_____

C. Does your personal vision reflect those values?

_____
_____
_____
_____

D. Are you living a life in which these values are being practiced?

_____
_____
_____

Insight   p. 69

Section 9

How Do You Measure Success?

I believe you will be greatly rewarded if you follow your heart. The rewards are different for everyone. We all have a guiding star. Find your star and you will fulfill your purpose. Success is being who you are. Successful people follow their heart. They believe in themselves. They have willpower and determination. They have a passion for what they do.

You have an inner guide that tries to lead you on your path. However, it's your decision – your own free will to follow it or not.

You need to tune into your natural abilities.

A question I am frequently asked:

>If the Universe is on my side, why don't I get what I ask for?

There are many reasons:

>You didn't ask the right person.
>
>You didn't ask for long enough.
>
>You shouldn't have asked in the first place!
>
>You didn't ask at the right time.
>
>You didn't ask for pure reasons.

Learn to tune into your natural abilities. Your world will start to vibrate when you hear the sound of your own drum. You must be in tune with the Universe – in tune with your mission on earth – in tune with your inner nature. You must be on "Purpose." The Universe can only give you what you are able to receive.

We are somehow "limited" in our potential to receive if we do not do what we are "made for." When we are not on "purpose" in life we <u>can't</u> receive what we are asking for. However, when we are on purpose then we are truly unlimited – successful!

Insight   p. 70

The Purpose of Life is to have a Purpose in Life – Discover Yours

Follow your inner urge. You are not a blank page. There is something written on your page. One of your tasks is to discover – "decipher" – what is written there. The earlier you discover what is written in your book, the more learned, accomplished and wise you can become.

The Universe will only support your true nature – Who you really are. The Universe only promotes what was written on that blank page. Your Purpose – Your Passion – Your Calling – Your Vocation. If you are a tennis player, play tennis. If you are a writer, *write!* If you're a mother, be the *best!* If you're a baker, *bake!* You know what you should be doing. If you feel you don't, now is a good time to find out. I guarantee you will be happier and life will feel right for you. Things will flow. There will be an ease to accomplishing your goals.

Questions you will want answered:

> Can I be successful if I am not myself?
> Can I succeed if I don't follow the natural flow of my personality?

Yes, if you are very disciplined and work hard – but not to the degree you would be if you followed your heart.

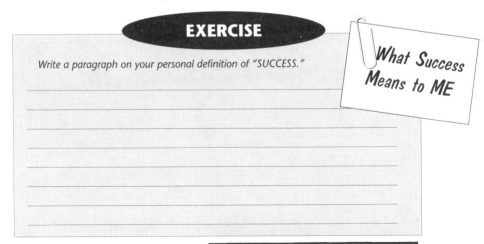

EXERCISE

Write a paragraph on your personal definition of "SUCCESS."

What Success Means to ME

Insight   p. 71

EXERCISE

Write a paragraph on what you would be doing if you were to follow your heart.

If I Followed MY Heart

Insight p. 72

Section 10

For Insight

The next three exercises are actually homework assignments. I think you will not only enjoy them but will gain valuable personal insight. You'll be learning a lot about yourself. You'll need this insight to implement changes in <u>attitude</u> and <u>behavior</u> that we'll cover in depth later.

EXERCISE

Spend a Day Completely Alone

I know this may be difficult to arrange, but it will be very worthwhile. Besides relaxing and reducing interaction and stimulus, a day alone will allow you to listen to you. Take along a notebook and write down your thoughts. Choose a setting that is peaceful and conducive to self reflection. Take along this book!

Where did I go to be alone?

What did I do?

What did I learn about myself?

What do I plan to do about it?

Insight   p. 73

EXERCISE

Spend a Day with a Child

Even if you have young children, this exercise is valuable to do with someone else's child. Giving full attention the entire day to interaction and conversation with a child might open your eyes and heart to your own inner child. Tell the child about your forgotten dreams and then listen. Children are amazing reflections of untapped possibilities, and have great innocent insight. The reason this is so powerful is that children have not bought into the idea that the world does not work. Take notes!

What child did I spend a day with? _____

What did we do?
_____
_____

What did I learn about myself?
_____
_____

What do I plan to do about it?
_____
_____

Spend a Day with a Senior

Borrow somebody's elderly parent or grandparent (again, not your own) or adopt someone from a nursing home. Share your questions, challenges, dilemmas and listen to the wisdom in return. You will get far more than you give, in both time and effort.

What senior did I spend a day with? _____

What did we do?
_____
_____

What did I learn about myself?
_____
_____

What do I plan to do about it?
_____
_____

For all the exercises above, remain in the present moment, but also monitor your behavior, reactions and revelations for further insight into **the hidden you**.

Insight   p. 74

Section 11

What's Good About My Life?

No matter how stuck in a rut you think you are, no matter how many things you'd like to change about yourself and your life, there are many positives besides the fact that you're alive!

Let's end this chapter on "insight" with the insightful exercise of making a list of 10 things (at least) that you are grateful for.

Keep this list where you can see it and add to it as you realize more reasons to be grateful. Count your blessings!

EXERCISE

10 Things I'm Grateful For

1.
2.
3.
4.
5.
6.
7.
8.
9.
10.

Insight   p. 75

Chapter 2 Review Page - Insight

Insight   p. 77

Insight p. 78

CHAPTER 3

"Personal Mastery/ Taking Responsibility"

CHAPTER 3 – TABLE OF CONTENTS

Section		Page
1	What Am I Responsible For?	83
	Exercise: Responsibility Questionnaire	86
2	Procrastination	87
	Exercise: MY Personal Procrastination Log	89
3	Design Your Future — Your Four Futures	90
	Exercise: I'm Taking Control of MY Life	91
4	Creating Your Preferable Futures	92
5	What Can I Live With/Without?	93
	Exercise: What I Can Live With/Without	93
6	Risky Business	94
	Exercise: MY Risky Business	95
7	How You Package "You"	96
	Exercise: MY Appearance	96
	Exercise: The New ME	97
8	Personal Energy	99
	Exercise: MY Energy Break	100
	Exercise: Anti-Boredom Measures	101
	Exercise: MY Personal Plan for Exercise	102
9	Body Language	103
	Exercise: Practicing Positive Body Language	104
10	The Power of Good Communication Skills	105
11	Dealing with Shyness	107
12	Eye Power	108
	Exercise: Eye Control of the Mind	111

(continued on next page)

Section		Page
13	Networking Skills	112
	Exercise: Personal Networking Questions	114
	Exercise: Professional Networking Questions	115
14	Networking for a Job	116
	Exercise: Network Directory Worksheet	118

Personal Mastery   p. 82

Section 1

What Am I Responsible For?

YOU are 100% responsible for what happens in your life! No excuses!

It's your choice – either (a) you take responsibility for your life, or (b) you are a victim of circumstances. When you blame circumstances or someone else, you give up your power.

> *START ACCEPTING RESPONSIBILITY FOR*
> *THE CIRCUMSTANCES IN YOUR LIFE.*

Know that you are an extremely powerful person – who has the power to create circumstances in your life.

> *YOU ARE RESPONSIBLE FOR HOW THINGS ARE NOW*
> *AND ARE ALSO RESPONSIBLE FOR CHANGING THE DIRECTION*
> *OF MANY ASPECTS OF YOUR LIFE.*

During your lifetime you may find yourself facing situations you have absolutely no control over. At these times, start saying, "I'm responsible and able to respond in the proper way to this situation. Simply because it directly affects me."

"The situation is just the way it is, and I plan to take care of it by finding a good solution." I'm not saying this is pleasant or easy. However, as a responsible, mature person you must do whatever it takes to move forward.

Just take responsibility and accept the situation.

Stop assigning a meaning to everything that happens. Just know that you have the power to assign no meaning or a new meaning to things that happen personally in your life.

Whatever happens in your life can only have the meaning you give to it.

The meaning you give to events makes no difference to the event. But the meaning you give makes all the difference to how you feel. (Think about this.)

Your power comes by accepting responsibility for what is. Once you understand and practice this you won't become overwhelmed – you will realize you are in control.

Everything depends on your perception of life's happenings. At times, things happen that are not pleasant and there is nothing you can do except ACCEPT them and take responsibility for them.

I'd like to give you a personal example of taking "RESPONSIBILITY."

My Grandmother came to America when she was five years old with her dad and brother Patrick. Her mom had died in Ireland. My Grandmother, Mary Donahue, was an immigrant from Ireland in the late 1890s. At that time in America, signs reading "Irish need not apply" were common. She married and became widowed with two small children. My Grandfather had started McCarthy's Funeral Home and, unfortunately, died at an early age. The night my Grandmother had buried her husband, someone knocked on her door and said they needed her husband. The person standing at her door had just had a death in his family. My Grandmother said, "I buried my husband this morning; however, I'll be right over." She walked from Saxonville to Framingham (five miles), borrowed some necessary things, and sat up and made herself a black skirt and jacket and conducted the funeral two days later. After graduating from college, my Dad took over the business, and McCarthy's Funeral Home is still in existence, being run by my two brothers.

Grandma did not stop there – Grampa and Grandma had a dream of owning their own home. Grandma did not allow that dream to die. She was living in a cold-water flat when she contracted to have a house built. The men she spoke with at first did not want to speak with her. They asked her to tell Mr. McCarthy to come down to speak with them. Every week she would walk over to the building site and pay them as they built her home. The house cost $4,500. I grew up in that home.

Personal Mastery   p. 84

The next dream Grandma kept alive and accomplished was to see her two children finish college. My Dad graduated from Boston College and New England School of Embalming, while my Aunt Mim graduated from Framingham State College and earned advanced degrees from Harvard and Boston University. Aunt Mim was a principal of a school in Framingham, Massachusetts, which now bears her name, "McCarthy School."

Grandma could have sat around and felt sorry for herself and hoped someone would rescue her, or have depended on others for support. She could have gone to work as a domestic, as many Irish women did, or work at the mill in town. Grandma wanted more. My Mom, along with bringing up five children, was also highly involved in the funeral business. She helped build the business and kept the books. As if this wasn't enough, she also managed Donahue's Pharmacy, which my family owned.

Let's take a lesson from Grandma, Aunt Mim and my Mom. I feel fortunate to have had such strong role models. I bet if you looked into your family history you would find a role model or two.

IT'S YOUR TURN
exercise on next page

EXERCISE

Responsibility Questionnaire

In what areas do I need to take responsibility?
_____
_____
_____

Actions I'll now take as a responsible person:
_____
_____
_____
_____

Areas in my life where I Blame Others; where I Blame Myself; where I Blame Circumstances:
_____
_____
_____
_____

Actions I'll now take as a responsible person:
_____
_____
_____
_____

Areas of My Life where I see myself as the Victim:
_____
_____
_____
_____

Actions I'll now take as a responsible person:
_____
_____
_____
_____
_____
_____

Personal Mastery   p. 86

Section 2

Procrastination

Why do people procrastinate?

Basic reasons:
- Lack of self-confidence in one's decision-making abilities.
- Lack of responsibility.
- Rebellion, resentment.
- Self-defeat; to sabotage one's self.
- Misperceptions of time.
- Fear of failure.
- Fear of success.
- Lack of goals.
- Lack of belief in one's ability to achieve.
- Feeling depressed.
- Not being focused.
- Feeling overwhelmed.
- Power play.
- Laziness.

How do I stop procrastination?

First Step: Self-analysis.
Know and **understand** why you procrastinate.

Second Step: Learn the correct techniques shown later in this book.
Know you **can stop** procrastinating.

Third Step: Understand that procrastination is a habit.

There are three kinds of people (we have all heard this):

      1. Those who make things happen.
      2. Those who watch things happen.
      3. Those who wonder what happened.

What category do you find yourself in? Come on, answer the question now.

A very common situation that triggers procrastination is being faced with an overwhelming task. Break such projects into small segments, according to importance.

If you continue to procrastinate, it will result in:

      1. Missed opportunity.
      2. Low productivity.
      3. Dissatisfaction with life.

I think it's important to remember that each of us has our own biological rhythms. Match your own peak physical and emotional time with high payoff tasks. Guard your peak hours for creativity. Use the other times of day for minor jobs that are necessary but less important to your success. Once you keep your activities in step with your biological clock, procrastination is easier to overcome.

How to deal with procrastination:

      1. Realize that you can stop procrastinating now.
      2. Admit it exists in your behavior.
      3. Take action to adopt the new attitude.
      4. Know that all you need to stop procrastinating is a firm commitment and the desire to do so.

Remember...this is a serious matter:

      it is bad for your self-esteem
      it makes you angry at yourself
      it causes stress, anxiety and fatigue

- it is wasting your time and energy
- it is costing you money
- it makes people not take you seriously

The good news is…once you stop procrastinating you will start achieving your goals.

EXERCISE

MY Personal Procrastination Log

What do I procrastinate about?

What has it cost me?

What do I plan to do about it?

Section 3

Design Your Future – Your Four Futures

A big part of taking responsibility is OWNING YOUR FUTURE!

What do you want your future to look like?

4 Futures = 4 Ps

> 1. **PASSABLE**
> Defeatist attitude – let things come at you and you'll accept them (taking no responsibility).
>
> 2. **PROBABLE**
> (Negative) It will look pretty much the way it has looked up to now. Nothing exciting – little to look forward to.
>
> 3. **POSSIBLE**
> Attitude that anything is possible (not committed; I suppose; low energy).
>
> 4. **PREFERABLE**
> What you want; you design it. Looking at all opportunities and options as positive alternatives – taking control.

I believe the future is not just "out there." You design it, you're the architect. The future is a potential. Please understand the past does not equal the future. Once you understand and accept that "where you find yourself right now is where you have positioned yourself," you can take full responsibility for how your Life looks and understand that you are capable of changing it.

THIS IS THE GOOD NEWS.

EXERCISE

Write what you would like your future to look like. Think about all the opportunities and options as possibilities.

I'm Taking Control of MY Life

Section 4

Creating Your Preferable Futures

Because there is often a time lag between your thoughts and their appearance in your reality, some people are reluctant to make the connection. Yet, you could trace every event that happens to people back to a thought, picture, emotion or belief they had at some point. Each and every decision and choice you make is shaping your reality in the present and the future.

Thoughts held in common by masses of people determine the way the world works. Understanding that the way you think affects the world you experience will help create positive changes in society. People must believe they have the ability to change their own reality for the better before they will believe they can assist in changing the world for the better.

You have many "preferable futures." There are many choices you can make about the kind of reality you can live in. There are thousands of realities you can choose from right now.

By picturing the world you would like to live in, you can create the reality you want to live in by imagining the best conditions you can, instead of focusing on negative conditions.

You can create your personal preferable future reality any way you want. Positive thoughts projected from your mind will go out to the future and meet up with you there!

DARE TO DREAM!

Section 5

What Can I Live With/Without?

The following exercise is designed to further help you figure out what you'd like to change, alter, or replace in your life – and I don't just mean things. I'm including behavior and associations, habits and attitudes. Part of being responsible involves making decisions on what you can/what you can't live without in your life.

EXERCISE

What I Can Live With/Without

What I can live with:

What I can live without:

Personal Mastery   p. 93

Section 6

Risky Business

Let's talk about risk taking. **What exactly is a risk?**

A risk is something that you engage in when the outcome is uncertain. Risks are an important element in your life if you choose to accomplish much. Playing it too safe does not allow you to grow to see what good stuff you are made of. It's important to take risks. If you never risk, you might as well mail in your life.

I have always been a risk taker. My Mom would say, "Tanny jumps and then looks to see if there is water in the pool." Being a little wiser now, I recommend people take <u>calculated</u> risks! There are times, however, when you must jump on blind faith. If you wait until you're really, really sure, you'll never take the training wheels off. You may end up with skinned knee's (I know I have), however, to go through life with the training wheels on is playing it too safe and that becomes boring.

When I speak of risks, I do not mean jumping off cliffs. One must understand and be ready to accept, and be able to live with, the consequences. When you risk, you always have the possibility of losing – you also have the possibility of gaining much! However, if you never risk, I feel you will never know what you are capable of accomplishing. Taking risks is exciting and challenging.

Most people forget as they are taking on new challenges just how difficult it is to let go of old habits. Intellectually you may understand that certain habits are holding you back – are even self-destructive. Please remember that your emotional memory will be whispering to you that it's not safe to take chances in your life. Even when you know rationally it's time to move forward and take a chance, a frightened voice inside may say "Wait, let's give this more time."

Acknowledge that frightened voice; however, you can't afford to let it keep you from moving forward.

Personal Mastery   p. 94

Holding back – holding on to what is familiar – is very common behavior. Getting out of your comfort zone is very difficult. You feel you are leaving a predictable, safe place.

There are no guarantees (life does not hand them out) that all will turn out as you wish. That's why it's "Risky Business" – please don't get upset with yourself for having fears, for wanting to turn back. However, DON'T turn back but remember: your freedom from your past is worth it.

Please remember, no one has ever died from being uncomfortable.

EXERCISE

MY Risky Business

Things I'm willing to take a risk on:

1.
2.
3.
4.
5.
6.
7.
8.
9.
10.

When was the last time you went out on a limb?

Personal Mastery   p. 95

Section 7

How You Package "You"

To attract – impress – the people/person you wish to attract, you must package yourself impressively. And it must show at first glance. "Your package" is what they see, what they judge you by. Your appearance is talking even when you aren't!

Your personal appearance makes a deep and lasting impression in people's minds. An unconscious "attitude" is formed either against you or for you based on what they see.

EXERCISE

MY Appearance

What is my appearance saying about me?

_____
_____
_____
_____
_____

Does my appearance project the image I want? ❑ Yes ❑ No

What image do I wish to project?

_____
_____
_____
_____
_____
_____
_____

Personal Mastery   p. 96

EXERCISE

What have I been neglecting about my appearance?

The New ME

CHECKLIST	WHAT I PLAN TO DO
☐ Wardrobe	
☐ Accessories	
☐ Hairdo/Cut	
☐ Nails	
☐ Makeup	
☐ Teeth	
☐ Weight	
☐ Posture	
☐ Speech	

Personal Mastery   p. 97

Because your appearance is so important, I suggest investing some time and money in an updated version of "you." The experts are out there, ready to advise you on current fashion, haircuts, weight control, nutrition and exercise to enhance your image.

CHECKLIST:

- ❑ Try a color analyst to figure out your most flattering colors.
- ❑ Try a chiropractor to improve your posture.
- ❑ Try a new hairdresser or barber for a fresh cut.
- ❑ Try a personal trainer for exercise.
- ❑ Try a teeth-whitening system.
- ❑ Try a wig or hairpiece or hair color.
- ❑ Try a professional massage for circulation/relaxation.
- ❑ Try a personal shopper through a department store.
- ❑ Try singing lessons to improve voice quality.
- ❑ Try a makeup make-over.
- ❑ Try a manicurist.
- ❑ Try a facial.
- ❑ etc._____

Section 8

Personal Energy

It's late in the afternoon: Do you know where your energy went? Are you drooping? Call it tiredness, fatigue, boredom, or lethargy, most of us run out of energy and wish we had more.

Sometimes fatigue has a specific cause, such as anemia, insomnia, depression or other illness, in which case you should consult your doctor. But there are many causes of tiredness that indicate a drain of energy. Since we pay attention more readily to physical aspects of our daily life, our levels of physical energy define our

"LIFE FORCE"

The critical importance of life energy has been recognized in many cultural traditions, and you may have heard some of the terms: the Chinese call it CHI, and it is also known as PRANA or the "breath of life." What is universally agreed upon is that the more PRANA or energy you have, the more vital your mental and bodily processes, giving rise to sound sleep, strong disease immunity, physical vitality and a sense of exhilaration. These are the <u>natural</u> qualities of human life when it is balanced and whole.

The body's main source of life energy is through <u>the breath</u>, which on a base level brings in oxygen, and on a subtle level brings in life energy. The ancient sages considered the quality of a person's life to be reflected in the quality of his breathing!

When breathing is refined, slow and regular, the circulation of life energy is reaching all levels of body and mind, promoting a state of complete balance. A healthy life demands:

- Fresh food
- Sunlight
- Free expression of emotions
- Pure water and air
- Moderate exercise
- Balanced, refined breath
- A reverence for life

Drink eight glasses of water each day, except when you exercise. Then drink more – before, during and after you exercise!

When body fluids fall below a certain level, a toxic state begins, which throws your brain chemistry out of balance and you'll feel lethargic.

Did you know that sitting for long periods of time can wear you out?

Intense mental activity can be more tiring than physical activity, using up incredible amounts of energy by directing your attention to one thing. Just be aware of this fact.

In addition, being sedentary and in poor physical shape without exercise means that every physical task requires even more energy – leaving you with less.

The solution is an exercise break. Even a 10-minute walk will break the fatigue routine and revitalize your energy level. Get up, move around, stretch and walk at intervals when you have been stationary for more than a few hours or so. If possible, walk outside. You'll feel refreshed and ready to work once again.

EXERCISE

I Will:

MY Energy Break

Personal Mastery   p. 100

Did you know a significant cause of fatigue is BOREDOM? If you are dead tired by mid-day, you may be losing your energy to a boring routine. I'll bet you'd find energy pretty quickly to do something you really love to do, such as going out to dinner or visiting a favorite friend. So, how can we avoid the energy drain of boredom?

EXERCISE

I'd like you to write a list of what I call "Anti-Boredom Measures" (things you know that perk you up):

Anti-Boredom Measures

Many of us force our bodies to keep going with endless activity on shortened sleep. Sleep debt accumulates and compounds. Studies have confirmed that adequate sleep improves alertness and energy levels. So, do yourself a favor and listen to your body.

Stress is definitely the number one cause of tiredness and fatigue. If you're going to beat fatigue, you have to learn to tackle stress (please see Chapter 4). Besides reducing stress every way possible, combat the physical tension it causes with...

    1. Relaxation techniques like deep breathing, yoga, Tai Chi, meditation, warm baths, or jacuzzis.

    2. Exercise.

Exercise is a great way to relieve stress and the tension it creates. Thirty minutes of moderate exercise a day is enough to gain major health benefits. The 30 minutes of exercise can include activities such as playing actively with children, dancing, vigorous housework, climbing stairs, brisk walks and even gardening. The trick is to find something you enjoy and do it!

Even though energy is used during exercise, IT CREATES MORE!

EXERCISE

(Only you know what you will commit to.)

MY Personal Plan for Exercise

Section 9

Body Language

Okay, now that your body is full of energy, what language is it speaking? Did you know that your body speaks volumes about your personality, attitudes and emotions? And, guess what...THE BODY DOESN'T LIE!

Think about it. When you feel depressed, how do you look? What do you do with your body? Are you standing straight and tall with a smile on your face? I doubt it. The shoulders slump, the neck is bent down, the eyes are not bright and clear – they tend to look down – and one tends to breathe shallowly. This does not allow much oxygen to go to your brain, so the cycle continues.

Each emotion you experience, feel, allow has a distinct pattern of its own.

EACH <u>ATTITUDE</u> AND <u>BEHAVIOR</u> HAS ITS OWN CORRESPONDING BODY POSTURE.

I would like you to be aware of the messages you send by how you stand, walk and sit. Please take time to observe yourself. By looking at how you stand, walk and sit you will be aware of how others see you. Your body language tells more about what you're thinking than you may be aware of. You often send out contradictory messages between your non-verbal and your verbal messages. The majority of people trust the non-verbal messages more than the verbal messages.

IT'S YOUR TURN
exercise on next page

Personal Mastery   p. 103

EXERCISE

Practicing Positive Body Language

All you need for this exercise is a full-length mirror and a chair. Walk in front of the mirror and take a good look at yourself. Ask yourself what you like and what you could improve upon. How is your posture? What is your facial expression saying about how you feel about yourself?

_____
_____
_____
_____
_____
_____
_____
_____
_____
_____
_____
_____

What has it cost me?

_____
_____
_____
_____
_____

What do I plan to do about it?

_____
_____
_____

Personal Mastery   p. 104

Section 10

The Power of Good Communication Skills

Communication involves both listening and speaking. Communication is influenced by experiential knowledge, values and expectations.

Experiential knowledge determines the understanding of the person on the receiving end of communication. What you can transmit emotionally to another depends on the person having experienced a similar situation. Trying to communicate what sadness is like is very difficult if the receiver has never felt sadness.

Effective communication depends partially on both sender and receiver having common experiences that allow non-verbal communication to occur. This merging is a sensing mechanism which forms a mutual or joint baseline for understanding what is being verbalized. There are certain baseline communications that are universal, such as expressions of happiness or grief. People who speak different languages can effectively communicate in these areas because they each sense what the other is conveying.

An important factor that influences communication is the set of values that the sender and the receiver of messages hold. What you believe in the form of biases and prejudices color show you hear what is being said to you. The internal process of going through the vast amount of data in your comprehension of what you receive is a very complex one that is subject to thousands of subtle attitudes based on your past experiences. You process messages in ways that are influenced by your values, beliefs and prejudices.

This is why two people receiving the same message will "hear" it differently since the message will be understood by one's individual set of emotions, experiences and thoughts.

<u>Your</u> <u>expectations</u> – determines how you communicate with another. Most people see and hear what they <u>expect</u> to hear and see.

You know examples I'm sure of people who have seen the identical scene and, when asked to describe what they saw, it was vastly different from the other person's description. You filter out both visual and auditory data that don't meet your <u>expectations</u> or needs.

Become a master of the spoken word. Become a forceful communicator. Use words to motivate people to take action.

Being able to communicate is an extremely important skill, one you need to develop if you choose to live well. You must develop the ability to deal with people. Please remember, we live in a world of words. Words are symbols. Everyone thinks with them. When you are speaking with someone, they are forming pictures in their mind. Their mind is a picture gallery. By our choice of words, you are helping the person project a mental image of what you wish him to see. His mind is like a blank canvas, so select the right words so he will clearly hear you.

Become a master of the spoken word, and you can cause someone to see what you wish her to see. You've heard the saying, "You certainly paint a pretty picture of things." Before you speak, master your own thoughts, and consider the power of your voice. Does your voice have a pleasing quality?

Have you ever listened to your voice and speech pattern on a tape recorder? If not, do so.

A powerful principle of personal interaction:

> Genuinely seek to understand another before being understood in return. True empathic communication shares words – ideas – information – feelings – emotions and sensitivity. It also assures the person that we accurately understand what has been said.

Section 11

Dealing with Shyness

New studies show that close to 48% of Americans think they are shy. Does that statistic include you?

Many things in today's society make it more difficult to be a social, communicative person. Ordinary, face-to-face contact with other people, such as the bank teller, gas station attendant and mail carrier have been disappearing – and along with them the development of social skills.

Social skills are very complex and include how to start a conversation, how to keep it going, how to give and receive a compliment, how to ask for proper service. These skills are not specifically taught in school – they are learned by observation, and there is less opportunity for that now.

More people live alone and come from smaller families with less interaction and entertaining on a social level. Automation and computer technology replace personal contact. Less interaction means less practice in socializing, leading to a higher number of introverted, shy people.

Shyness can be a safeguard against risk and rejection, and it can become crippling. Basic to overcoming shyness is building self-esteem, something I am helping you to do in this book.

Here is a short list of reminders for building self-confidence, for those of you who feel you are shy:

1. Recognize you are unique; assess your strengths.
2. Never say bad things about yourself.
3. Stop overprotecting your ego.
4. Forgive yourself for mistakes, embarrassments and failures.
5. Don't tolerate people/situations that make you feel inadequate.
6. PRACTICE being social.
7. Develop long-range goals.

Section 12

Eye Power

What I call "EYE POWER" is the ability to

Keep a Quiet Mind

It's your first step to power...the power to manage yourself, manage others and manage your life.

A quiet mind in a crisis is like the "eye" of a hurricane – the devastating winds are violent except in the center (the eye) of the hurricane, which is *completely calm* – in the very center of the destructive forces all around it.

Your own eyes must be like the "eyes" of hurricanes because in every emotional storm, your eyes must be the center of absolute calm. It is the absolute calm of your relaxed eyes which is the unusual method of keeping a quiet mind.

Learn to control your "mind-moods" (emotions) by eye relaxation:

> There is a very close relationship between your eyes and your mind. This action/reaction between your eyes and your mind includes, but is much greater than, physical vision.

Are you aware of the fact that your eyes are highly emotional? They respond to your emotions and they stimulate or relax your mind-moods. This goes beyond physical vision (outer vision).

Eye emotion directly affects *inner vision* (mental pictures and mind-moods).

> So, it's to your benefit to learn to <u>control your eye emotions</u>!

First, understand how your eyes respond to your mind-moods (emotions)…

Your eyes have quite a story to tell!
Your eyes weep in grief – your eyes smolder with resentment
– your eyes flash with anger – dance with excitement.

"If looks could kill,"…"smiling eyes,"…blank stare of a disturbed person, …shifty eyes,…fire in your eyes. Your pupils enlarge when you're interested,…they flutter when you flirt,…flame with hostility. Your eyes are the windows to your soul, people roll their eyes in disbelief, eyes widen with excitement, squint with disbelief or questioning, burn with desire, show envy, show desire,…a twinkle in his eye.
Watch those eyes.

Want to know what someone is thinking? Watch their eyes. A baby will cover his eyes if he doesn't want to hear something.

When your eyes respond to your emotions, they stimulate and escalate the emotions to which they are responding and which they openly express.

By relaxing the intensity of your eye emotions, you can calm the mind-moods (emotions) themselves. This is the first step toward achieving a quiet mind.

Eye control of mind-moods is accomplished by:

- Becoming constantly aware of the emotions which your eyes are expressing, realizing that tense eye movement stimulates and escalates the mind mood itself. Conscious awareness enables you to focus on your emotion, so you can relax it with the restraint of mind control induced by eye relaxation.

- Relax your eyes simply by mental command – *by deliberately causing your eyes to feel relaxed*. "Blank out" all eye tension.

- Make your eyes feel blank. Imagine your eyes having a "blank look," unemotional, completely relaxed, almost asleep.

- When your eyes are completely relaxed, they absolutely cannot stimulate, escalate, or sustain uncontrolled emotions. It is psychologically impossible to feel two directly opposite emotions at the same time. So, by completely relaxing your eyes and "blanking out" all eye emotions, you *turn off* the high-tension emotions that are damaging to you.

So much of your life is controlled by the universal Law of Consistency…If your eyes smolder with resentment, your mind-mood also will be resentful. If your eyes smile with love, your mind-mood will be filled with love. <u>Your emotions always</u> will be the same (consistent) throughout your entire nerve system.

For the same reason (consistency), by RELAXING your eyes, you relax your mind-mood so that you cannot feel tense. And because you cannot feel tense, you cannot feel or express high-tension emotions. You simply *turn off* tense emotions when you relax your eyes.

So, when you begin to feel tense…

STOP – **CLOSE YOUR EYES!**

You will feel more physically, mentally, emotionally relaxed. You will achieve one of life's most rewarding and satisfying goals – *a quiet mind*. **Give yourself this gift.**

EXERCISE

Eye Control of the Mind

What times will I set aside each day for eye relaxation?

In what situations would eye relaxation be helpful?

Section 13

Networking Skills

Networking often is FREE FORM. It's not about attending specific seminars or workshops (although those are good places to network). Networking is a 24-hour-a-day proposition.

It's an attitude toward business and life in general.

Networking is helping others get what they want, ultimately leading to *our* getting what we want. It's giving so we can ultimately get. It's a **WIN-WIN SITUATION!**

Those who give the most invariably get the most.

What else can I do for you?
What can I do to help you?

Your success will depend in large measure on the extent to which you help other people get what they want.

SIX DEGREES OF SEPARATION

The principle that any person on earth is separated from any other person by, **at the most**, six people.

This principle is directly related to networking. In other words, YOU can "get to" any person you want to. YOU know someone who knows someone who knows someone who knows **the** person you want to make contact with.

Suggestion:

Purchase Bob Burg's book, "Endless Referrals" (McGraw-Hill).
Excellent book!

WHY NETWORKING WORKS

#1 It's built on <u>reciprocity</u>. I help you and you help someone else, and someone else helps me. Sometimes the person you help <u>never</u> helps you <u>directly</u>, but indirectly, you'll benefit from everyone you help. Networking works in harmony with the way "Life" works.

"What goes around comes around."

#2 It's built on professional <u>friendships</u>. People like to help and do business with people they consider trustworthy, honest, decent <u>friends</u>. <u>People</u> associate with people they like and trust.

#3 It takes advantage of the "Law of Averages." It's a numbers game. The more contacts you have in your network, the more success you'll enjoy. The bigger your network, the greater your success.

"Fish where there are fish."

If you want lobster, don't go to freshwater bays – you can set a thousand lobster traps and you will never catch a lobster. Go where the best lobsters are – ice-cold, saltwater.

RULES FOR EFFECTIVE NETWORKING

1. Let <u>everyone</u> know your line of work, hobbies, interests.

2. Help others get what they want. Networking is a two-way street. "Help and you will be helped."

3. Network at <u>all times</u>. Network even when business and your social life are good. Don't wait until down times before cultivating contacts. The time to build contacts and network is <u>ALL</u> THE TIME.

4. Subtlety is the key to networking. Don't push too hard. Be friendly in your approach.

5. Network outside your specific fields of interest. You never know who'll be able to help you.

Personal Mastery

6. Keep track of your networking contacts – business cards are valuable – keep an updated Rolodex/phone book...This is *"gold."*

7. <u>Sincerity</u> is a key part of networking. Nobody likes a phony. Express a <u>genuine</u> interest in those people you're coming in contact with.

8. <u>Don't</u> keep score when you network. Give unselfishly. Don't be a "soft touch," but don't hold back when you can help.

9. <u>Start giving people less of what they don't want</u>. People are very aggressive in avoiding what they don't want in their lives. Even more so than in getting what they want. You don't want to be associated in people's minds with something they don't want.

10. Start attracting favorable attention of those who can lift you towards your goal. How? Start demonstrating your willingness to first help them to accomplish whatever it is they are trying to do.

11. Follow up – always do what you promised to do ASAP.

12. Never do business while networking.

<u>Look continuously for "new ideas" that will be of value to people</u>. (Think creatively, use your imagination, be an idea person.)

EXERCISE

Personal Networking Questions

Build a strong personal network. Person/people I have fun with:

Person/people I can count on:

Person/people who push me to grow:

Personal Mastery   p. 114

EXERCISE

Professional Networking Questions

Person/people I have fun with:
_____
_____

Person/people I can count on:
_____
_____

Person/people who push me to grow:
_____
_____

Build your life around this. Make yourself valuable to people.

Most people do not think in this manner. Most people are only thinking of ways to get what they want. Stop being preoccupied with what you want.

Keep in mind: People are <u>not</u> interested in what you want.
People <u>are</u> interested in what <u>they</u> want.

In order for people to give you what you want, you must first give them what they want.

1. Find out from each person who is important to you what they want – ask them.

2. Let them know you'll give them what they want or help them get it.

3. If people don't know what they want, help them figure it out and help them get it.

Personal Mastery   p. 115

Section 14

Networking for a Job

Your most promising route to a job you love is through the power of networking. Once you've put together a list of contacts, what do you say to them? Every networking conversation is different, but here are some basic guidelines:

Tell them (briefly):

1. Why you're contacting them.
2. About your background.
3. About the career/job you hope to find.
4. About where you've applied and what resources (e.g., agencies) you've used so far.

Ask them:

1. Would you be willing to give me names of people who might be able to advise me about my job search? Ask if you can use your contact's name; then, when you call, you can say, "So-and-so suggested that I call you because…" (If you feel comfortable doing so, you might also ask if your contact will call ahead to introduce you.)
2. Would you give me names of people in your organization, or in organizations you're familiar with, so I can send them resumes? Again, ask if you can use your contact's name and, perhaps, if your contact will introduce you.
3. Do you know of any meetings I could attend?
4. If you were me, who else would you talk to?
5. Where would you look for published job openings (newspapers, magazines, libraries, databases, in-house bulletin boards, etc.)?

Personal Mastery   p. 116

6. If your contact works at a company you're interested in pursuing: Does your own company have an in-house bulletin board of job postings? Would you be willing to check that board for me?

7. Are there any employment agencies you'd recommend? Any you'd avoid?

Leave them with:

1. A copy of your resume (so they'll know how to get in touch with you or be able to pass it on, if appropriate).

2. Your thanks – and don't forget to follow up with a thank-you note now, and again when you do get the job.

3. A promise that you will return the favor in the future.

Then:

1. Keep the names, addresses, telephone numbers of job contacts on a personal computer system, index cards, or flip chart paper.

2. Create a tickler system so you remember to follow through with your promise to re-contact them.

3. Use a network directory worksheet for each contact (example on following page).

EXERCISE

Network Directory Worksheet

\# _____

Name: _____

Tel. (home): _____

Relationship: _____

Profession: _____

Home Address: _____

Company: _____ Tel. (office): _____

Address: _____

Date Called: _____

Referred by: _____ Referral's Tel.: _____

RESULTS: _____

• New Names: _____
_____

• Other Appointment: _____

• Other Info (co/industry): _____

FOLLOW UP: _____

• Letter: _____

• Call: _____

COMMENTS: _____
_____
_____
_____
_____
_____

Personal Mastery   p. 118

FORMAL NETWORKING

Prepare yourself mentally before attending a network meeting by setting goals.

Example:

1. To gain potential business leads
2. To leave with at least three solid new contacts
3. To help three people with their wants or needs
   - Always arrive early.
   - Bring plenty of business cards.
   - Wear a name badge if they are available.
   - Target key people. Introduce yourself; ask how you can help them! Ask for a business card.
   - Look for people you know. Introduce them to appropriate people.
   - If you're hungry, eat right before, so you won't have to balance food and a drink.
   - Make eye contact. Shake hands.
   - Move around.
   - If your spouse or friend is with you, instruct them ahead of time of the type of person/people you wish to meet.

Hints:

   Start with people you already know.
   Don't drink.
   Don't sit.
   Don't leave early.

After you network:

   Do what you promised.
   Keep in touch.
   Edit your contacts.

Chapter 3 Review Page-Personal Mastery/Taking Responsibility

Personal Mastery   p. 121

Personal Mastery   p. 122

CHAPTER 4

"Understanding Stress"

CHAPTER 4 – TABLE OF CONTENTS

Section		Page
1	Identifying Stress	127
	Exercise: Identifying Stressors in MY Life	129
	Exercise: How I Handle Stress	130
2	Making Sense of Life's Changes	131
	Exercise: MY Transitions	132
3	Letting Go	133
	Exercise: Meditate to Relieve Stress	134
	Exercise: Letting Go	136
4	Getting Through Life Changes	137
	Exercise: MY Life Changes	138
	Exercise: Facing Tragedy	140
5	Handling Rejection	141
	Exercise: Handling Rejection	142
6	The Stress of Loneliness	143
	Exercise: Positive Steps	144
7	The Stress of Mistakes and Failure	145
	Exercise: MY Mistakes	146
8	The Stress of Anger	147
	Exercise: MY Unhealthy Anger	148
	Exercise: My Healthy Anger	148
9	Whatever Happens, There Are Only <u>Five</u> Things You Can Do	149
	Exercise: MY Responses	152
10	A Simpler Life	153
11	Life Too Stressed? Simplify, Simplify	155
	Exercise: MY Diary	157

(continued on next page)

Section		Page
12	The Seasons of Your Life	158
	Exercise: MY Winter	159
	Exercise: MY Spring	160
	Exercise: MY Summer	161
	Exercise: MY Fall	162
13	SAD (Seasonal Affective Disorder) Adds to Stress	163
	Exercise: MY Action Plan	164
14	Tanny's Stress Busters	165
	Exercise: MY Personal Stress Busters	169
15	Where's Your Sense of Humor?	170
	Exercise: MY Plan for Laughter	172

Understanding Stress   p. 126

Section 1

Identifying Stress

We all live with stress in our lives. Most of us feel stress in one form or another almost daily. Let's examine its symptoms – and form strategies for managing it. Let's look at the causes and how to manage or eliminate it.

There are two types of stress, according to clinical psychologist William D. Brown, Ph.D., in his book, *Welcome Stress! It Can Help You Be Your Best*:

1. "EUSTRESS," from the Greek "eu" meaning "good," is the type you can convert to positive energy, the type that can motivate you to be active and to achieve your goals. All stress is not bad; if there were none, there would be no vitality. A "dynamic tension" is good for you to a point; then it turns toxic. The anxiety-laden kind, the overload, is what we refer to as "DISTRESS."

2. "DISTRESS," from the Latin "dis" meaning "bad." (The Good Sisters of The Holy Cross would be proud of me. I did remember some things from four years of Latin.) This kind of destructive stress is mostly self-induced. The behavioral signs include:

(Check those that apply to you)

- ❏ Difficulty in relaxing
- ❏ Difficulty in slowing down
- ❏ Indigestion
- ❏ Responding in anger to minor irritations
- ❏ Nervousness
- ❏ Critical attitude toward others
- ❏ Fatigue
- ❏ Inability to focus attention
- ❏ Loneliness
- ❏ Overeating
- ❏ Excessive smoking
- ❏ Drinking more
- ❏ Sleep disturbances
- ❏ Constant feeling of being overwhelmed
- ❏ Lack of sense of humor
- ❏ Headaches
- ❏ Feelings of despair
- ❏
- ❏ Aching neck
- ❏

Do you recognize some of these symptoms as yours? Once you do, you can begin to deal with the causes – and be in better control.

Understanding Stress   p. 127

Dr. Estelle R. Ramey, a nationally known endocrinologist, has long studied the effects of stress on the life expectancy of humans, as well as rats. What she found in both species is that the ones who have CONTROL OF THEIR LIVES live longer. Those whose circumstances are perceived to be out of their control are more likely to succumb to a stress-induced death.

She states, "It's not hard work that kills. It's not competition. What kills is not having control over your life."

Everyone has a different level of stress tolerance, but three factors cause distress:

1. **Lack of Predictability:** A constant state of vigilance and anxiety.

2. **Lack of Control:** Inability to change, either events or your attitude about them.

3. **Lack of Outlets for Frustration:** Inability to release pent-up tension, emotion, worry, fear, etc.

It is interesting to note that there would be little stress without the <u>memory</u> of previous stress, for our memories dictate our responses. We feel out of control and frustrated whenever a situation reminds us too closely of an earlier time when we were out of control and frustrated.

STRESS BECOMES A SELF-FULFILLING PROPHECY!

There are a few simple stresses in human life because as soon as a new event occurs it is natural that the imprint of old memories becomes activated, triggering the kind of stress we <u>anticipate</u>. I'll give you methods to counteract that anticipation later in the chapter.

You should be <u>aware</u> of the amount of stress factors in your life.

The following is a list of some life events that often cause distress, especially when combined. Humans can withstand extraordinary stress, but if we are pushed too far, our stress response turns on our own bodies and begins to create breakdowns, both mentally and physically.

Identify your stressors by checking the box next to each life change that you are currently dealing with.

EXERCISE: Identifying Stressors in MY Life

- ❏ New career
- ❏ Loss of employment
- ❏ Retirement
- ❏ Move
- ❏ Change in financial status
- ❏ Bankruptcy
- ❏ Menopause
- ❏ Birth, becoming a parent, grandparent
- ❏ Child leaving home
- ❏ Child moving back home
- ❏ Death of partner
- ❏ Death of relative, close friend
- ❏ Divorce, marital breakdown
- ❏ Separation
- ❏ Becoming a step-parent
- ❏ Remarriage
- ❏ Operation
- ❏ Serious illness
- ❏ Major accident
- ❏ Large debts
- ❏ Travel
- ❏ Vacation
- ❏ Holidays
- ❏ Family gatherings
- ❏ Incarceration
- ❏ Conflicting goals
- ❏ _____
- ❏ _____

If you've checked even one life-changing event, you need coping mechanisms and a support system. Let's assess what you already have available to cope with stress.

Understanding Stress   p. 129

Do you really know how to deal successfully with the stressors in your life? Do you handle things with a sense of control, knowing that you can cope? Or do you tend to fall apart and become nervous and hopeless about your situation? Many people who are going through life changes manage to handle the stress and cope successfully.

EXERCISE

How I Handle Stress

Coping mechanisms I currently use:
_____
_____
_____
_____

Support systems I have to help me:
_____
_____
_____
_____

Understanding Stress p. 130

Section 2

Making Sense of Life's Changes
"Surviving Transitions"

What most people usually resist is "transition," not change.

Change occurs when something new starts or something old ends! And it takes place at a particular point in time.

Transition cannot be localized in time that way, since it is the gradual psychological process through which individuals reorient themselves so they can function and find new meaning in a changed situation.

<u>Change</u> often starts with a new beginning.

<u>Transition</u> must start with an ending.

It's a letting-go process. Unmanaged transitions are likely to lead to unmanageable changes. Change and transition differ in another way. In change, the new replaces the old immediately. In transition, there is a limbo state – a "no man's land" – between the old reality and the new one. In this in-between state, neither the old rules nor the new rules work, even though one or the other may be officially in place. Everything feels confused, empty, meaningless, a "neutral zone."

Managing the ending that a change will entail is essential. It's important to be careful of yourself – between the old and the new. It's a disruption of the status quo and is an extremely stressful time.

The good news is it's a source of renewal and creativity.

New beginnings happen when the transition process gets to the point where they are ready to happen. It's important for you to know and understand how transitions affect you:

There is <u>pain</u> in <u>endings</u>, <u>confusion</u> in the <u>neutral zone</u>, and <u>excitement</u> for the <u>new beginning</u>.

As a human being, you must understand that your subjective world is shaped by certain elements. You must look at:

1. Personal history
2. Collective history, cultural values
3. Your temperament (how you perceive and evaluate experiences)
4. The phase of life you are in

Most people take a long time to let go of old beliefs, old patterns.

EXERCISE

MY Transitions

What transitions am I faced with right now?

What positive steps can I take to make this easier for myself?

Understanding Stress   p. 132

Section 3

Letting Go

Most people find letting go painful. Why is letting go so difficult? What steps can we take to make the journey through this process easier, less painful, so we can find new beginnings?

Life hurts at times, as we all know. Letting go is often like grieving a death, but rarely do we consider it as just that. We all must deal with loss throughout our life. Every "yes" to one set of circumstances means "no" to something else. The first day of school, leaving high school, going away to college, marriage, moves, job change, deaths, lost dreams – on and on, loss after loss. We must expect them. The smart thing to do is to expect them and learn how to handle them. So the question is: How do we know when to keep trying, when to hang on, and when do we let go?

I have a tendency to operate on feelings; however, emotions are not always a reliable barometer. It's great to have feelings and be a feeling person, but I've learned it's not wise to always act on them. Learn to allow yourself some time to think and meditate on a life decision that you must make.

Have you considered meditation? It is much more than a relaxation exercise. Besides clearing your thought processes for decision making, meditation can neutralize stress. Levels of cortisol and adrenaline, stress-released hormones, are found to be lower in long-term meditators, and their coping mechanisms tend to be stronger than average.

Meditation has profound effects on the body, all positive! If you haven't tried it, here are the basic techniques:

EXERCISE

Meditate to Relieve Stress

1. Pick a brief phrase or word that reflects your basic spiritual belief or a positive thought.
2. Sit in a comfortable position, relaxed but not to the point of falling asleep.
3. Close your eyes.
4. Relax your muscles. Start with your feet and work your way up to your neck and face, letting each muscle lose tension and relax.
5. Become aware of your breathing. Breathe slowly and easily, through your nose. Breathe in, and as you exhale, silently repeat your focus word or phrase.
6. Clear thoughts from your mind gently. Picture stray thoughts, worries, problems floating away inside balloons. Picture a blank screen if it helps.
7. Continue breathing slowly, repeating your phrase or word as you exhale for a set period of time, at least 10 to 20 minutes.
8. Practice the technique at least twice a day. When you wake up in the morning and before you go to sleep are ideal times. During the day if you feel the need, try to give yourself the time.

There are no side effects of meditation except peace, reduction of stress and a clarity of mind. Try it!

Understanding Stress   p. 134

STAGES OF LETTING GO

Being the daughter of a funeral director, I was constantly exposed to how people handled the loss of loved ones. I learned from my Dad how difficult a time this is for people and have always been sensitive to it. We all have an initial reluctance to letting go. Eventually, we realize we must do it. Whether it's the loss of a loved one, a destructive lifestyle, loss of a job, or of a material possession, loss of health, youth, a friend. Letting go is a process. This process, like any other process, works itself out in stages. It is an extremely personal time, and each person goes through the stages at a different pace.

Stage I: The realization hits. We become numb. This is a normal reaction, it's a coping mechanism. Without this protection, some situations are so painful one would lose control. Your hopes and dreams become shattered. The happiness you had is shattered. Stage I is especially difficult if the loss is misunderstood or if it's denied by people close to us. If the loss is not expressed, shared and talked about, it stalls the healing process.

Stage II: We pretend all is well. We believe if we pretend everything is okay, it will be. We try to re-assert control over something that is out of our control. We are in denial. We go about our daily business in a robot state. We may look and act as if we are "doing just fine;" however, we are not even close to being ourselves.

Stage III: We mourn. This is a time of loneliness. We believe that what we had was better than anything the future could bring. We believe we will never be happy again. It's imperative to take the time to mourn the loss. Understand it's part of the mending process. Cry, do whatever you need to do.

Stage IV: A gradual feeling that maybe just maybe there may be some hope for future happiness again. We begin to design our view of ourself and our future. Acceptance does not mean forgetting what happened or pretending it doesn't hurt. Acceptance means saying goodbye to what we had and beginning to design a new life.

Stage V: Last stage. You begin to feel stronger and at the same time a little shaky. At this time you must stay in the game and have faith that tomorrow will be better. In crises lie new opportunities for becoming all we were meant to be. These are tough times. Take the grief, the loss, and build a bonfire. Sit and watch it. Burn up all of the trivial concerns and clutter that has been in your life. It's time for the song, "I Think I Can Make It Now."

EXERCISE

Letting Go

What must I let go of?

What stage am I in?

What can I do to help myself move forward?

Section 4

Getting Through Life Changes

Some stages are brief. Sometimes, going through a stage takes a long time. Give yourself the required time.

Just as a broken arm takes time to mend, so does saying goodbye. You need time to mend. Be gentle with yourself, allow yourself what you need. You wouldn't expect to be 100% with your arm in a cast; well, think of your emotions with a cast on them as needing protection from life. This is where friends can be of great help. A good friend listens, doesn't judge, isn't solicitous, does not tell you everything is fine. He/she just listens and is there for you.

Many people find it helpful to write a letter or poems or start a journal. Some put their feelings on tape. The point is to express your feelings, get them out in whatever form you're comfortable with. Little by little, small cracks of light will start to peek through the black.

It's important to know you're not alone.

Fifteen million Americans are members of over 500,000 support groups. They are people helping people through difficult problems by listening and affirming. "Emotions Anonymous" is one group you may want to look into. Your local church or synagogue or hospital will have the names of support groups near you. Once you start to believe you can once again trust, true healing begins. Many people find the best antidote is to help others who need help. We don't honor the dead by dying with them. My Mom told me before she died to remember she had a good life and at the times when I would miss her to find someone less fortunate than myself and help that person. She told me, "Life is for the living." She gave me a medal before she died that said, "Always look forward and never look back." This has worked for me. When I start to feel sorry for myself losing my Mom, Dad, sister and dear friends, I help someone who is still here who is going through a tough time. It always makes me feel better.

Understanding Stress   p. 137

People do not heal quickly from personal loss. There is such a thing as being "heartbroken." It doesn't mean you're ill or that you're condemned to be chronically depressed. It means you need time to recover. It's a time to be good to yourself, you need and deserve it.

EXERCISE

MY Life Changes

What life changes am I faced with at the present?

What can I do to heal?

FACING TRAGEDY

When tragedy comes into your life, you have to face the truth and face the way things really are. This is a time you must admit you're in crisis. When you hear the news of a tragedy, you have to realize that the damage has already been done. No matter how hopeless the news is, you have to accept it. You must tell yourself that you're in a severe situation, and take action if it's required. You must accept the cruel facts that directly affect you. This is your reality. Until you own it, you can't work on solutions. The best you can do sometimes is exercise <u>damage control</u> and accept the crisis.

When tragedy comes, you have no choice but to accept it as reality, and work things out. Once you face the conflict, you feel a tremendous sense of relief. The problem hasn't left, but a solution can be sought. It's a time you must be strong. I'm not saying this is easy. It's your worst nightmare coming true. Reality can be cruel.

The process is not easy. We many times ignore things that are painful – a feeling of hopelessness sets in. Some situations won't go away or change. By not addressing them, they will actually multiply and spill over into other areas of your life if left unattended. Worrying about something won't change the facts. The best thing to do is to regroup, take an honest look at your resources, <u>ask for and accept help</u>. Once you start the process, you can begin to rebuild your life. It's tough to cut your losses; however, you're ahead of the game to see clearly where you are and what steps must be taken.

What is needed are <u>tough</u>, <u>healthy</u> choices. There are times you are <u>forced</u> to <u>let go</u>. You don't get a vote. There is definitely a therapeutic value to working through your problem. You must move forward. You will be in pain and experience depression. However, you will transcend the emotional crisis – time does heal emotional scars.

Understanding Stress   p. 139

If you find yourself facing a tragedy, I wish to offer my sympathy. Loss is difficult and painful.

A book I would highly recommend is by Rabbi Kushner, "When Bad Things Happen To Good People." Avon books.

EXERCISE

Facing Tragedy

What tragedy am I facing?

What healthy choices must I make?

Section 5

Handling Rejection

Many stressful life changes involve rejection: separation, divorce, loss of employment, etc.

> Your reaction to the rejection is not based on what has happened, it is based on how you process that information.
>
> It is impossible for someone to create feelings of rejection in your emotions. When you experience rejection, it is because you have lost control of your emotional system.

Although you may not be able to control the stressful event, or your body's reaction to it, your appraisal, the vital link that bridges the event and the reaction, is UP TO YOU.

The totally personal way in which we filter events determines how stressful they are. External stressors like rejection are TRIGGERS. If you don't feel triggered, there is no stress. What stresses us out isn't the life-changing event so much as the negative perception we create of it.

Stress always arises if you have expectations about how something HAS to be. (*Example:* You HAVE to stay together; you HAVE to keep that particular job.) How you handle rejection, which is part of life, is extremely important.

IT'S YOUR TURN
exercise on next page

Understanding Stress   p. 141

EXERCISE

Handling Rejection

When have I felt rejection?

How did I react?

What can I do that would be more helpful to me?

Understanding Stress   p. 142

Section 6

The Stress of Loneliness
Loneliness is the Number One Disease in America

Loneliness is definitely a stressor – like pain, loss, injury, grief and fear. Physiologically, loneliness can trigger stress responses. It can be traumatic, altering the production of hormones, which, in turn, alters the function of many other systems in the body.

Ultimately, every cell in the body can be affected, causing cardiovascular diseases (such as heart attacks, strokes, migraine headaches), autoimmune disorders and asthma. The body's healing capabilities will also be affected.

Loneliness recognizes no boundaries – it crosses all gender, ethnic and socio-economic barriers. Just being around people is often not enough to prevent loneliness. It is the quality of the relationship that determines whether you feel lonely.

Factors that can lead to loneliness include illness, disability, loss of employment or change in family structure, or loss through death or divorce, social pressure to juggle multiple responsibilities, frequent moves, etc.

A real relationship of any kind is a form of psychotherapy that can reduce the stress of loneliness. And that includes a relationship with a PET!

We covered "your network" of personal and professional people in an earlier chapter. It's your responsibility to build these for your emotional health.

EXERCISE

What positive steps could I take to be less lonely? (Suggestions: join a club, volunteer your time to a worthy cause, adopt a pet)

I will:

Positive Steps

Understanding Stress   p. 144

Section 7

The Stress of Mistakes and Failure

Our errors, mistakes, failures and our humiliations can be terribly stressful. There is even the problem of repeated mistakes and failures. If someone's mental or spiritual condition is not right, often he becomes error-prone, triggering additional regret and stress. Mistakes and failures can, however, be looked at as great TEACHERS instead of as stressors.

As serious as you feel they are, every mistake has positive aspects. It is a developmental experience for one thing – something that helps you grow and become more mature. The fact you've made a mistake indicates you've taken a risk, which is a good thing. Every decision carries with it the risk, the anxiety of failure, yet inaction is almost always worse than wrong action!

Mistakes and failures, instead of being stressors, can be a means to an end ...and not an end in themselves. When they have served their purpose, they should be forgotten. If we consciously dwell upon the error, or consciously feel guilty about the error, and keep berating ourselves because of it, the error or failure itself becomes the "goal" which is consciously held in our imagination and memory. Stop reliving the past over and over in your imagination, continually criticizing yourself for past mistakes. Stop beating yourself up.

IT'S YOUR TURN
exercise on next page

Understanding Stress   p. 145

EXERCISE

MY Mistakes

Write down the really serious mistakes you feel you've made in your life:

What can I learn from these that will help me in the future?

Section 8

The Stress of Anger

Recent work in psychotherapy shows the difference between healthy and unhealthy anger. Healthy anger happens only briefly, usually at the moment you feel violated in some way. It can give you strength and energy to deal with the problem at hand. It leaves you feeling better, not more angry. It's not a chronic condition.

Unhealthy anger is both a symptom and a cause of stress. There are two types of unhealthy anger:

1. <u>Misplaced anger</u> covers up real emotions, such as worry, hurt or guilt. It is chronic, and people seem to get no relief from expressing it. It keeps us from solving real problems.

2. <u>Manipulative anger</u> covers up a desire for power. It is intimidating, addictive and dangerous.

Unhealthy anger is best handled through therapy, since it is rarely acknowledged as inappropriate by those who exhibit it. Exhibiting unhealthy anger often causes extreme stress in those around you. It's up to you to avoid such people.

However, healthy anger need not be a stressor but a friend. Anger in itself is a sign that something is wrong and needs to be fixed. When directed to productive (instead of destructive) action, it can relieve frustration and stress.

EXERCISE

MY Unhealthy Anger

Is unhealthy anger a problem for you?

What are the issues, and who or what is affected by these?

What do I plan to do about it?

EXERCISE

MY Healthy Anger

Do I have healthy anger?

What is it trying to tell me?

What do I plan to do about it?

Understanding Stress   p. 148

Section 9

Whatever Happens,
There Are Only <u>Five</u> Things You Can Do

You can usually choose your response to stressful situations – most times, the choice is yours! *Understanding the choices* is extremely important.

Since the choice is yours, the responsibility is also yours. By understanding the five responses, you will be prepared to respond successfully to each situation presented to you.

The five responses are:

      (1) Over-response

      (2) Under-response

      (3) Delayed Response

      (4) Non-response

      (5) Unexpected Response

Each type of response can be used successfully, and each can be disastrous, depending upon your ability to choose the most effective response to use in each situation and your skill in using it.

How to use them effectively is vitally important to your success in life.

Let's learn *why*, *when* and *how* to use each response and, equally important, when <u>not</u> to use them.

THE FIVE TYPES OF RESPONSES

1. **Over-response:** What can we say good about over-response? Very little – over-response is anger, fear, panic. It intensifies the problem. You can't win by over-response; it's to your disadvantage to over-respond. It's like an overheated engine that will eventually blow a vital part. Very energy draining – it's being constantly up-tight.

2. **Under-response:** Does not take life and its irritable people and circumstances too seriously.

   Under-response gives you control, power; an advantage of under-response is that you retain the option to apply increasing pressure later if needed.

3. **Delayed Response:** Patience, power.

   The best results are obtained by first considering all possible alternatives, then choosing your course of action once you have the facts. Throughout your entire life, you will be confronted with very few emergencies which require instant action.

   Important and complex decisions which involve many alternatives and detailed analysis, including your seeking expert advice, will require time.

   Do not allow yourself to be pressured, into taking action. Be suspicious of anyone who will not permit you time to consider alternatives and consequences.

4. **Non-response:** Times you choose not to respond at all, you are using a deliberate kind of response, known psychologically as "non-response." Many times, the most effective response, the most successful response, is no response at all.

   Many times, we initiate trouble by our unnecessary involvement or over-involvement or unnecessary reaction or over-reaction when no response may have been the best choice.

   It is not necessary that you do something just because somebody asks you. You can deliberately choose to do nothing. Start to include this in your list of alternative choices. Just because someone expects you to do something does not mean you must do it.

5. **Unexpected Response:** The art of doing the unexpected can be used in any situation. The next time something or someone irritates you, instead of reacting in a manner that they would expect from you surprise them. You will surprise them. This can be a lot of fun and very creative. You will catch people off guard and lighten up tense situations.

IT'S YOUR TURN
exercise on next page

EXERCISE

MY Responses

1. Over-response 2. Under-response 3. Delayed Response
4. Non-response   5. Unexpected Response

Now that I understand the five responses available to me...

- What response or responses do I mostly use?

_____
_____
_____

- What responses work well for me?

_____
_____
_____

- What responses should I start to use more?

_____
_____
_____

- What specific situations could use new responses from me?

_____
_____
_____

Promise to me:

STOP, THINK OF WHICH RESPONSE WILL BE APPROPRIATE FOR THE SITUATION, AND IMPLEMENT IT.

Understanding Stress   p. 152

Section 10

A Simpler Life

Has being in the fast lane gotten you where you wish to be? You wouldn't be alone or out-of-step to consider scaling down, simplifying your life.

Simplifying life means working smarter, working less, working differently and living differently.

Instead of dropping out of their current lifestyles, many people are opting out of the pressure of a high overhead and the 40-plus hours a week required to pay for it. It can be an equitable trade-off giving up some of your paycheck and material things for extra time with family, friends, and R & R.

Simplifying your life can start with small things, such as shopping less for items only wanted instead of needed, and avoiding upgrading or keeping up with the Joneses. Do you really need a bigger TV or a newer car or another pair of shoes? Probably not.

Is it really necessary to have and read stacks of magazines and newspapers, which thrive mostly on disaster and bad news? Limiting access to negative information can really contribute to a sense of peacefulness. Don't worry, you won't miss out on the important news.

Eliminating luxury vacations, extravagant restaurants and expensive gift giving will scale down that budget and help eliminate financial stress. People work for things not pleasure these days, and your things such as houses, cars, credit cards CAN OWN YOU!

For some, scaling back has less to do with money than with quality of life versus quantity. For some, it means fitting everything they own into only a few boxes. For others, it means giving up the headache of home ownership for the freedom of renting. Selling your big house and renting a smaller

Understanding Stress   p. 153

one, or a condo instead, allows you to call the landlord when something goes wrong. It also allows you the freedom to move with less hassle.

Having doesn't mean *owning* anyway when you are a ransom to the bank for the house, cars, boat, computer, etc. Many people are finding it refreshing to get off the treadmill of trying to impress others with where they live and what they drive. Simplifying can put you in the enviable position of living for yourself and your family and not for the sake of someone else's opinion.

Simplifying life and scaling down one's lifestyle is not a matter of choice for some. Poor health, a failed marriage, ailing economy leading to job loss, all force an evaluation of priorities.

A drastic change of lifestyle may happen against your wishes and certainly opposite your life plan, but shifting gears to a simpler life is not all that bad. Living with less status, stuff and stress can get you in better touch with yourself, your loved ones and the natural environment.

Moving out of a highly materialistic world can be a culture shock at first. It may take therapy in addition to patience and the support and understanding of family and close friends to make the transition. Going from being a highly-paid executive workaholic with a half-million dollar home and two cars to working at home as a consultant out of a modest home may take many steps, some uncomfortable. But there are always advantages to be gained and counted. The former executive now has only steps to commute instead of an hour in traffic, and he can enjoy most of his meals with his family. Your general physical, emotional and mental health will improve.

In an ironic way, catastrophe which precipitates a scaled down lifestyle can enable you to regain yourself in the long run. A good attitude about changing to a simpler way of living will empower you and enable you to be happier, healthier and certainly more creative! It's an option to think about.

Understanding Stress   p. 154

Section 11

Life Too Stressed? Simplify, Simplify

Feel rushed?

Frantic?

Feeling pulled in too many directions?

Not spending time with people you care about?

Feel scattered?

Not getting to do things you enjoy?

The merry-go-round you have put yourself on separates you from yourself. Maybe it's time to get off...STOP. Time to sort out the "too much" and put a plan in place that is comfortable to you.

Let's start:

Why do you want to simplify your life?

What do you believe it will bring you?

What do you mean by a simplified life?...less to do?

...less confusion?...less pressure? Less responsibility?

The definition of a "simple lifestyle" is a consciously directed life – with clear goals. It does not mean taking the easy way. It does mean living for what we most love and living a life expressing our deepest values.

If you want something different, you must understand this involves change. You will have to have the courage to change and take action.

How did your life become so complicated? They were all your choices.

Is trying to be a perfectionist a problem for you?

Is not saying "No" something to consider?

Is wanting to be liked your weakness? (Want approval.)

Understanding Stress   p. 155

Are you too concerned about other people's opinions?

Do you constantly compare yourself to others? (Bad habit – they either depress you or puff up your pride.)

Do you lead an overstimulated life? (Constant noise, activity, conversation.) (Look at the voluntary stimulation in your life – and cut back on it.)

Are you overly driven – pushing yourself unrealistically?

The cause of complications seems to be "our heart and soul unsettled" in the way we are living.

We lose who we are, what we want. Become confused with what we really love – and don't know what the purpose of our life is. We haven't taken the time to get to know what our deepest desires are. We lack focus and don't seem to have goals in our lives, a "Life Plan."

You must simplify your inner life before your outer life can become calm and stay under control.

How you live now is what you must look at honestly!

EXERCISE

MY Diary

For one week track everything you do — how you spend your time. Your diary should be very insightful as to how complicated your life has become.

Day 1

Day 2

Day 3

Day 4

Day 5

Day 6

Day 7

Understanding Stress   p. 157

Section 12

The Seasons of Your Life

Notice each one of us has seasons, and they are very personal. Recognize what season you are in. Some are for learning, some are for doing, some are long, some are short.

YOUR PERSONAL LIFE – *Analogy to Nature*

YOUR LIFE is like the seasons in New England. You can't change the seasons, <u>you can only change yourself</u>. Learn to adapt and find beauty in each. Take from each the best it has to offer. Try to be ready for each the best you can and understand each will be different. You can count on the fact that they <u>will come</u> and <u>they will go</u>. Some are easy, some are difficult. Some are short, some are long. Whatever season you are in, <u>be in it</u>, try to understand the lessons, what you can take from it to build on, what you can <u>do</u> to prepare next time.

WINTER:

What can you do about these months of your life? Winters won't change simply because you want them to. You must meet the challenges they present to you. The winters of your life are difficult times. Know they will come. With winter storms sometimes you get a warning and can prepare. Sometimes they come unexpectedly and are disastrous. These are the times in your life when dreams get smashed, when it seems you just can't win, when everything is difficult.

The winters of your life can be both *external* and *internal*. It's a time when you must tough it out. Know it will pass, but take the time to examine what happened. What lessons did you learn? There are always lessons. If you don't learn the lesson, *it will be given to you again*. You will become stronger from living through it – so assess the damage and get ready for spring.

Understanding Stress   p. 158

EXERCISE

MY Winter

What winter storm am I weathering?

What do I plan to do about it?

What are the lessons?

SPRING:

It's a wonderful time of the year. Everything comes alive. There is movement all around. The world seems to be waking up – the trees blossom, the flowers bloom and the birds appear and delight us with their songs. Take advantage of the springs in your life. ***Opportunity always follows difficulty***. You can count on it, just as day follows night.

Spring is a time for a fresh start. It's a time to get busy. Spring is a time to plant new ideas, make new plans, get rid of the damage from the winter. Time to clean up your act. If you are doing the right thing, making the right choices in the spring, your fall will be rewarding.

Spring is a time to open the windows of our mind and let our imagination soar. Each one of us gets a handful of ideas and opportunities. They come to us, at times, in subtle ways. Be aware, be ready. Take advantage of them.

Be open to them. When you get one idea or opportunity, check it out. Recognize it, seize it, develop it, plant it and protect it. They may be small, like seeds that have the potential of becoming magnificent flowers just coming to life. Be careful, you may trample it and it may be gone forever. All you need is **one** that you can hold on to.

BE OPEN-MINDED. SPRING IS LOADED WITH POSSIBILITIES. A TIME TO LOOK AT YOUR FUTURE. Spring may have rain showers. Enjoy them. Without rain showers, there can be no rainbow. It's time to build your own rainbow.

EXERCISE

What opportunities or ideas do I have to take advantage of?

_____
_____
_____
_____

What am I open to? Am I ready?

_____
_____
_____
_____
_____

MY Spring

SUMMER:

Summer in New England is a wonderful time. It's a time to work and protect what you have planted in the spring. It's a time to be vigilant. Just like the crops and flowers you planted in the spring, the ideas and projects you started you must now protect. Understand all good gets attacked. In the world of plants, it's weather conditions and insects. In the world of ideas and opportunities, there will be things you cannot control, such as economic conditions or poor timing. People also must be a consideration; some will be in competition, some are merely distractions, some will be negative and some do not wish you to succeed. Be mindful of these facts.

Understanding Stress p. 160

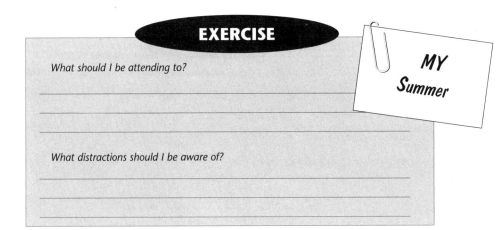

FALL:

FAll is my favorite time of year. It's a time to enjoy the benefits of all the hard work you've done the three seasons before. What you had weathered in the Winter, planted in the Spring and keep nurturing all Summer is now ready to be harvested. This is an exciting time, it's a time to reflect on what it took to bring you to this place. The choices you made, the seeds you planted that were so small are now in full bloom. If you made good choices and were vigilant you should have a bumper crop. Whatever you have sown you now may reap. Those who were not as vigilant will have less to harvest than you. Enjoy your successes without apology to anyone. This is a time to say to yourself "job well done." Fall is also a time for giving thanks and to prepare for Winter. Just as the squirrels and other animals start to prepare for the Winter, so must you. The more prepared you are, the better you will winter the storms.

EXERCISE

MY Fall

What will I have to harvest?
_____
_____
_____

What can I be proud of? What can I enjoy?
_____
_____
_____

Understanding Stress   p. 162

Section 13

SAD (Seasonal Affective Disorder) Adds to Stress

Are you a little depressed when winter rolls around? Do you experience low energy levels, headaches, irritability, crying spells, craving for starchy foods? You may be experiencing symptoms of Seasonal Affective Disorder. It is an extreme form of the winter *"blahs"* and may adversely affect the motivation and energy level you need to work on your goals. People living in areas with distinct seasonal changes such as New England are especially prone to SAD.

The cause of SAD is not known but it may be linked to the body's biological clock that controls temperature and hormone production.

Many people associate different moods with different seasons. Some, however, experience full-blown episodes of *"SAD"* or *"winter depression,"* beginning in the fall and subsiding in the spring. It is marked by oversleeping, overeating and carbohydrate craving. People who have SAD also tend to suffer from daytime drowsiness.

It is clearly associated with a decrease in the amount of daylight as the days grow shorter because it disappears spontaneously as the days lengthen. Phototherapy (light therapy) is used to treat depression resulting from SAD and is extremely effective.

A patient undergoing phototherapy sits a short distance from a bank of special lights much brighter than normal indoor lights. The exposure to intense light appears to work best either early in the morning, when it is still dark outside, or in the evening. This suggests that light therapy may work by tricking the biological clock into thinking the day is longer than it is.

People undergoing phototherapy often notice improvement in their SAD after just two or three days of treatment, and it has no notable side effects.

If possible, take a vacation to a warm climate for a week or even a long weekend. Another suggestion is to go to a hotel or health club that has a heated pool and lots of glass. On sunny days the sun pours in and feels good on your body. You may also simply sit in a room in your own home where the sun is coming in. ***Get outside each day.*** On days that the sun is not shining you will still benefit from the ultraviolet light. Lastly, bring some outside indoors during these cold months. Plants and flowers placed around your home will not only help the quality of the air you breathe but will also lift your spirits.

EXERCISE

Things I can do to help myself during the winter months:

MY Action Plan

Understanding Stress   p. 164

Section 14

Tanny's Stress Busters

**My Number One Stress Busting, Coping Suggestion is
ADJUST YOUR ATTITUDE!**

Please don't allow stress to be a permanent condition in your life. One thing in life we can count on is that things, circumstances, people in our lives, etc. change. How you deal with change is critical to your well-being.

Positive attitudes will carry you through the toughest days. Negative attitudes are destructive. Negative thoughts limit your chances for happiness. Negative thinking patterns actually lead to physical and emotional problems. Mind-Body connection is real. A positive mental attitude is the single most important trait toward achieving happiness and maintaining a healthy body. Dr. Deepok Chopra has done great work in the field of mind-body connection. I recommend you read all of his books.

Happy, optimistic people seem to have an abundance of natural internal opiates, called endorphins, secreted and used by the brain.

The presence of endorphins actually causes the feeling of well-being. Studies show clinically depressed patients have a severe lack of the chemical endorphin. Behavioral researchers are learning that we can actually stimulate the production of endorphins through optimistic thoughts and positive attitudes. Negative thinking robs the body of endorphins, leading to depression, which leads back to more negative thinking.

Let's reverse the process:

Positive Mental Attitude creates a natural high which helps people to overcome depression, turns stress into energy. Positive thoughts produce endorphins. Endorphins, in turn, encourage feelings of optimism and well-being. These feelings reinforce positive attitudes.

You are responsible for your actions and attitudes. People who are happy, satisfied with themselves, and successful in getting what they want from life are self-made. Their positive attitude makes them what they are.

A positive attitude is important for everyone.

Enthusiasm is contagious. It's difficult to remain neutral or indifferent with positive thinkers around. He/she radiates energy, good humor and motivation. It's important for you to be around positive, upbeat people.

YOUR ATTITUDE IS A CHOICE YOU MAKE.

What can you do?

Learn to control your thoughts – think positive. You can change.

You are in charge of your life.
You are in charge of your attitude.

How you think and how you react is totally up to you. Looking for bad things to happen can actually make them happen.

OPTIMISM IS A LEARNED ATTITUDE!
AVOID PESSIMISTS! MISERY LOVES COMPANY.

You are the programmer of your attitude. How you choose to program it will work for or against you. Whatever your goals are, their direction is set by your attitude. You choose for them to be self-enhancing or self-destructive. Your attitude creates the outcome according to your instructions. During difficult times, until a solution is found or the situation changes, you'll survive. Your inner optimistic attitude shines through to your outer behavior which the world sees.

You are not responsible for what happens out there, what others do or think. You are only responsible for how you choose to respond.

That's your attitude. The responsibility is yours.

Stress results from feeling out of control. A very simple way to regain control I have practiced is to:

MAKE LISTS

Your brain is a magnificent computer, but sometimes you'd be better off to write it down. Relying on memory when you have a complicated, stressful life will only add to the strain. "To-Do" lists relieve stress immediately.

Writing down what you have to do relieves pressure. Why? Instead of trying to keep track of what you have to do, with a list you can focus on what must be done and cross off items once you do them. This gives you a feeling of moving forward and accomplishment.

SET PRIORITIES

Taking a few moments at the end of each day to set priorities for the next day allows you to decide what to spend energy on, and in what order.

Another stress buster is to:

SCHEDULE BREAKS

A break can be as simple as a change of activity. Even a five-minute break can relieve stress and give you more energy.

A few more stress busters to keep on your schedule:

1. **Exercise**

    Physical activity enhances your body's use of oxygen, releasing those endorphins that temporarily cut through depression.

2. **Diet**

    Diet plays an enormous part in how you feel. Eat smart and be careful with alcohol. Definitely stop smoking.

3. **Drink More Water (Pure Water), 8-10 Glasses a Day**

   Water provides the hydration necessary for conducting electrical impulses throughout your body. It improves concentration, improves mental and physical coordination. It flushes toxins out of your system.

4. **Massage**

   A massage is a great stress reducer. Find a good massage therapist or learn how to give your partner or yourself a massage. There are great products on the market to make this a pleasurable experience.

5. **Get Enough Sleep – and Dream**

   Sleep requirements vary. Most people feel better when they get between 7 and 8 hours. Getting enough sleep each night assures that you will go through the levels of sleep that are restorative. A good night's sleep helps you face life's challenges in a positive mood.

6. **Develop Hobbies**

   Distractions from stressful situations are healthy. Make sure you take the time to enjoy them. Participate in pleasurable activities.

7. **Take Yearly Vacations**

   Not having lots of money is no excuse for not taking a vacation. There are lots of reasonable fares and things to do within one's budget.

8. **Take Mini-Vacations**

   A mini-vacation can be a day trip or something as simple as turning your phone off and ignoring the world for a day.

9. **Spend Time with Those You Love**

   It's important to share time with people you care about. Physical contact leads to emotional stability.

10. **Pamper Yourself in Little Ways**

    Be good to yourself. Buy yourself a book, go see a movie, go out for dinner, meet a friend for lunch, take a walk on the beach, or window shop. Do whatever makes you feel good.

Stress is extremely threatening to your well-being.

However, stress <u>can</u> be positive. It can cause you to take action, and it provides extreme amounts of energy. It's either a positive or negative experience. ***Use it to your advantage.***

EXERCISE

MY Personal Stress Busters

What do I do now to reduce stress?

What will I start doing?

Section 15

Where's Your Sense of Humor?

Laughter triggers physiological changes in the body that may help ease pain. Laughter induces the brain to release catecholamine hormones which release endorphins, which are the body's natural pain killers.

Laughter provides relief from stress. Much research in this area is being done by Dr. William Fry, Jr. of Stanford University.

Suggestion:

> If you don't have a sense of humor, develop one! Find out what makes you laugh and smile. Learn to use humor as an escape. Even serious situations have a funny side. Look for it. Many times in life you can either act depressed or laugh. Choose to laugh. Learn to laugh at yourself. Make light of your shortcomings or weaknesses that you can't change. Take defects and exaggerate them.

Use humor to diffuse difficult situations. You will set the tone. This is true in personal, as well as professional, settings. I know humor works. I run a networking company which is very successful. Important business is accomplished and the people also have fun. I use humor to bring out the best in each person.

Don't be afraid to relate funny stories. The world needs it.

Humor adds spark. It electrifies. You will find that people will seek you out.

Find friends, people who are upbeat.

Laughter is contagious.

Smile – it improves your face value. You'll feel better. You'll confuse people.

Think happy thoughts.

Understanding Stress   p. 170

Let your silly side out.

Make time to have some fun every day.

Encourage laughter in your home.

Once again, many adults have been programmed not to laugh or smile from childhood. Do you remember being told in school, "Wipe that silly grin off your face! What do you find so funny – would you like to share it with the class? Act your age! This is not appropriate behavior. I don't see any humor in that." If you went to Catholic School, as I did, being silly was not acceptable behavior. As a matter of fact, you were given a slip if you were caught talking in the halls.

Let the child out again. If it has died, bring it back. Find out what makes you smile and laugh. This is a personal matter. There are all types of humor. Make a list: Things I enjoy...Things that make me smile...Things that make me feel happy...People I enjoy. Movies – books – toys (yes, I said toys, you're allowed!) – CD's – clothes – videos – places – be playful. Collect humorous sayings, jokes. Go to a playground, swing. Be around young children.

You will become more creative, less rigid and more willing to try things.

I have a sign in my office: "Smile when you walk in this door."

Write a new philosophy for yourself, to see the world as a wonderful place filled with opportunity and joy:

> "I will find the time to laugh, smile and find humor in difficult situations. I'll let the child in me out and be a kid again. I'll work on changing my attitude, put things into perspective."

> "I'll stop wasting precious moments and feel I've cheated myself if I haven't made time for fun each day."

> "I owe this to me for my mental health."

EXERCISE

MY Plan for Laughter

Write down what you plan to do to lighten up:

Understanding Stress   p. 172

Chapter 4 Review Page - Understanding Stress

Understanding Stress   p. 174

Understanding Stress   p. 175

CHAPTER 5

"Setting Goals"

CHAPTER 5 – TABLE OF CONTENTS

Section		Page
1	Mastery of Goal Setting	180
	Exercise: MY Goal Experience	182
2	A Clear Purpose	183
	Exercise: Identifying Purpose	184
3	Goals or Gleams?	185
	Exercise: MY Gleams	185
4	Beware of Ghost Goals	186
	Exercise: MY Ghost Goals	186
5	Goals as Motivational Tools	187
	Exercise: Why I Haven't Set Goals	188
6	My Life Line	189
	Exercise: MY Life Line	190
	Exercise: MY Life Review	191
7	Creating the Life You Desire	194
	Exercise: Goal Visualization	195
8	Current Reality and Revising Goals	200
	Exercise: Working Towards MY Dream	200
	Exercise: MY Goal Experience	203
9	Making Things Happen	205
	Exercise: Identifying Positive/Negative Forces	206
10	The Big Picture	209
11	Your Personal Goal-Setting Plan	211
	Exercise: MY Specific Goals	211
	Exercise: MY Action Steps	213

(continued on next page)

Setting Goals   p. 178

Section		Page
12	Your Planning Wall	214
13	Become a Goal Setter	218
	Exercise: MY Goals	220
	Exercise: A Goal for MY Success	221
14	Scared Free	222

Setting Goals   p. 179

Section 1

Mastery of Goal Setting

Do you ever wonder why setting goals is the starting place in almost every course, book or tape that discusses success or achievement?

Without goals, we are on a trip without a destination. I'm sure you would not start out on a trip without a destination. Most people plan more for their two week vacation than they do for the most important trip they will ever take – **"Their Life."** You can't expect to reach the destination you want if you don't have a plan (a road map). This is what goal setting will do for you – it will guide you and assure your success in reaching your dreams.

Almost everyone you ask will tell you they have goals, such as "I want to be happy. I want to be rich" or "I want to have fun." But are those really goals? The answer is no. Some people call their daily "to-do" list their goals. And others call objectives goals. Whatever terms or definitions are used, the fact remains that we as humans need to focus on a specified result.

Why Don't We Live by Our Goals?

Given that nearly everyone has some awareness that having goals is a good thing to do, why don't we live our lives by our goals?

1. WE WERE NEVER TRAINED IN THEIR TRUE IMPORTANCE. How many goal-setting classes did you have in high school or college? How much training have you had in learning to focus on a specific result and adjusting daily to insure attaining it?

    We are aware that most successful individuals operate from goals. And yet, it is estimated that only between 1% and 3% of us set written goals. How sad.

Setting Goals   p. 180

Setting goals is a key area in which we must be committed to ongoing learning. We continually need to learn new methods and expand our understanding of functioning so that we achieve our goals.

2. FEAR OF CRITICISM is the second reason we don't live by our goals. I'm sure you have had the experience of being excited about something you decided to do, only to be told how it couldn't be done, or how silly it was. Most people have a negative response to any new idea and are quick to let you know they don't think your idea will work.

   Don't let negative responses affect you. Move ahead. Your motivation will suffer much more for not trying than if you go for it and don't succeed. Keep in mind that their response is only an opinion.

3. FEAR OF FAILURE is the third and primary reason we do not set goals and manage ourselves to make them happen. It is deeply ingrained in many poeple's subconscious. They have been trained to think and feel that failing is not acceptable. In truth, *there is no failure.* There are only lessons.

   Success, like most things in the physical universe, is a numbers game. Each failure brings you closer to a win.

   Thomas Edison had over 5,000 "failures" before he found the right combination to make the light bulb work. Had he succumbed to failing, he would never have had patented 1,095 inventions – more than any other person.

   Babe Ruth struck out more than any other ballplayer of his era – he also hit more home runs.

   MAKE A COMMITMENT TO SUCCESS. NEVER GIVE UP. Each "failure" is a new lesson you will use to succeed.

   Acknowledging and letting go of past incompletions in meeting goals will propel you forward in this new goal-setting process.

EXERCISE

MY Goal Experience

List some goals you set in the past and never accomplished.

Write your negative feelings about setting goals.

Setting Goals   p. 182

Section 2

A Clear Purpose

Goals exist within a hierarchy. At the base of the hierarchy is *purpose*, followed by goals, planning and scheduling. Each progresses from the one below it.

GOALS COME FROM PURPOSE. Plans come from goals. Scheduling comes from plans and, in turn, leads to success!

This systematic method will provide the formula necessary to make your goals a reality. Success is a reflection of how consistent you are with your purpose and how many goals you have realized.

LIKE SUCCESS, PURPOSE IS INTANGIBLE. It is a statement of your desire and the foundation for your goals.

The key to achieving your goals, therefore, is in defining your purpose. To become good at goal setting, you must do it.

Setting Goals   p. 183

Let's consider your purpose in each of three key areas of your life: Talents/Career, Relationships with Others and Self-Development. Some examples of phrases you might include in your purpose are:

> continued good health
> expanding physical strength
> emotionally stable and secure
> financially independent
> continued happiness
> fulfilling relationships
> making a contribution
> an expression of talent
> nurturing work habits

Remember, a purpose is not measurable; it is intangible and ongoing. It is an expression of your higher self.

EXERCISE: Identifying Purpose

My purpose in the development of my TALENT/CAREER is:
___

My purpose in the development of my RELATIONSHIPS WITH OTHERS is:
___

My purpose in SELF-DEVELOPMENT is:
___

Having a clear view of your purpose will provide you with an overview for setting your goals.

Setting Goals   p. 184

Section 3

Goals or Gleams?

STATISTICS SHOW THAT HIGH ACHIEVERS OPERATE FROM CLEARLY WRITTEN GOALS that are believable and attainable.

Goals are tangible, measurable, attainable and include a completion date. Goals support your purpose. Goals are results we are committed to producing. If it is a goal, it means you are going to take action on it.

It is important to separate your goals from your "gleams."

"Gleams" Are Different

- Gleams are desires you have not committed to yet.
- You are not able or willing to develop plans for them or schedule time.
- Gleams are very important.
- Your gleams list contains desires and dreams.
- Gleams will become goals when you give the time, energy or resources to commit to them.

EXERCISE

MYs Gleams

You are not yet ready to make a commitment to these ideas (will consider at a later date?):

Setting Goals   p. 185

Section 4

Beware of Ghost Goals

Ghost goals – what are they? These are ill-defined, non-specific goals that are too vague, that will never become a reality for you. For example, saying, "I want a lot of money" does not create a clear picture of what you want. Saying, "I want two million dollars in three years" is clear. Your subconscious mind needs clear, specific directions.

EXERCISE

My Ghost Goals

What have I been fooling myself about wanting?

Setting Goals   p. 186

Section 5

Goals as Motivational Tools

<u>Goal setting is an important self-motivational tool</u>. When you commit yourself to the accomplishment of your daily goals and you follow through on your promises to yourself <u>day after day</u>, you begin to trust yourself, believe in yourself, and feel in control of your life.

Remember: <u>Each day</u>, do something that moves you forward to reaching your goals. (Even baby steps count.)

You cannot do anything in the future; you can only do things in the present. Make today count.

PLAN YOUR FUTURE GOALS AND DO YOUR DAILY ONES.

Once you commit yourself to your goals and you begin to see results, you activate a very important force that will propel you to your goals – ENTHUSIASM.

Why Goals?

1. <u>It's important to have goals</u>. You are making life choices for today that will affect your future.

2. <u>Setting goals is a way to get things moving</u>. (We all get stuck.)

3. <u>It's important to give direction to your energy to determine how you can best spend your time</u>.

4. Goals are your <u>yardstick to measure your progress</u>.

5. <u>Goals are motivators</u>. Goals help you stay focused and let you keep score. Reached goals propel you forward to do more.

"Go for it!" "Make it happen!"
"How much do you want it?"

Setting Goals   p. 187

You will never get "it" until you know what the "it" is. The first step to success in any activity is the formation of <u>specific</u> goals. You would not take a trip without knowing your destination, but many people go through their lives without any definite goals. It is as simple as this: If you do not know where you wish to go, how will you know you've arrived?

The Power of Goal Setting

We are all naturally goal directed. Whether it is a satisfying lifestyle, a nice home, love, money, or status symbols, we always strive to fulfill our wants, needs and dreams. Once you direct and focus attention on specific, meaningful goals, you unleash your innate potential. Once you commit to and have a burning desire to reach your goals, you will tap what psychologists term **"your hidden reserves"** – the physical, psychological and emotional resources that <u>you have that are seldom used</u>. These hidden reserves are responsible for peak performance in people who accomplish great things.

EXERCISE

Why I haven't set goals in the past:

- ❏ Never realized their importance
- ❏ Didn't know what my goals were
- ❏ Did not know how to set goals
- ❏ Too lazy
- ❏ Fear of criticism
- ❏ Fear of failure
- ❏ Fear of success

Why I Haven't Set Goals

What has it cost me?

_____
_____
_____
_____
_____
_____
_____
_____

Setting Goals   p. 188

Section 6

My Life Line

1. On the following page, <u>draw a line</u> to represent your life. Begin at the bottom of the page at your birth. <u>Indicate on the spiral where you are NOW</u>.

2. Write the *key* events or happenings in your life, starting with events as early as you can remember and proceed to the present.

3. Leave space between years – you will find that one memory triggers another. Move back and forth above the line as the memories start to flow.

4. Ask yourself the following questions about each key event, and put the appropriate symbol after each one.

        a. Was this event negative, stressful?   Symbol = N

        b. Was this event positive, happy?   Symbol = P

Take your time.

5. Then answer the "Life Review" questions as you refer to your completed life line.

Setting Goals   p. 189

EXERCISE

Draw a line from your birth to your death and show where you are now. Write the key events of your life, indicating P (positive) or N (negative). **Assignment: You may also want to do this on a large poster board.**

MY Life Line

DEATH

(Write where you are now, and your age)

BIRTH
(Your birth date)

Start ———●

Setting Goals   p. 190

EXERCISE

MY Life Review

Life Choices (positive/negative)

Positive Choices   *Benefits I Enjoyed*

1.   1.
2.   2.
3.   3.
4.   4.
5.   5.

Negative Choices   *Costs to Me*

1.   1.
2.   2.
3.   3.
4.   4.
5.   5.

Refer to your Life Line Chart.

PAST LESSONS LEARNED:

1.
2.
3.
4.
5.
6.
7.
8.
9.
10.

Setting Goals

HOW DO I FEEL ABOUT MY LIFE AT THIS POINT?

WHAT DO I WISH TO ACCOMPLISH WITH THE REST OF MY LIFE?

Setting Goals   p. 192

Most people do not formally set goals; however, everyone has a dream. When your dreams have a specific plan of action, you are starting to use the powerful system of ***goal setting***. Goal setting can transform your fantasies into realities. Just as great buildings are conceptualized as blueprints, your life also needs blueprints or plans.

YOU ARE THE ARCHITECT.

Do you envision an ordinary structure or something fabulous? The following rules will provide a solid foundation on which you can build your dream:

1. **Write down your goals.** This process will start to make your dreams more concrete.
2. **Make your goals personal.** Goals are most meaningful when they are what you want for yourself.
3. **State your goals in the positive.** Concentrate on what you want, not what you do not want. "I want to win" is much more powerful than "I don't want to lose."
4. **Make your goals ideal but real.** For a goal to be effective, it must be believable to you.
5. **THINK BIG.** The bigger the goal, the more motivational value it has.
6. **Challenge yourself.** The sky is the limit. "A person's reach should exceed his grasp." Stretch – see what you are made of.
7. **State your goals as specifically** as possible. Crystal clear...elaborate on the details.
8. **Give each goal a specific completion date.** Know what it will look like when met.
9. **DO IT NOW.** Answer the questions in the next section to begin your personal goal setting plan.

Setting Goals   p. 193

Section 7

Creating the Life You Desire

"Turning your dreams into reality"

Creating is a skill that you can not only learn – you can master! Creating is a skill that is accumulated.

"The more you create, the easier it is to create."

By creating, I mean *bringing a desired result into existence.*

- ✓ **Conception** When you know what you want, you can more effectively create what you want.

    What do you want to create in your life? more of? less of?

- ✓ **Vision** From a general idea to a specific idea of the result you wish...make it specific, tangible, clearly defined.

On the following page, define your vision-goal. Write down a brief description of what you want your life to look like. Write down your short-term and immediate goals with a brief description and dates. This will help keep you focused. It will let you see how you're doing. Track your progress.

Setting Goals   p. 194

EXERCISE

Goal Visualization

WHEREVER YOU ARE NOW IS WHERE WE'LL START
Sit down. Pick a quiet spot. Shut your eyes. Give yourself time.

STEP 1: Relax – bring yourself to a reflective frame of mind.
Define your vision-goal. What do you want to create of yourself and the world around you? (This requires a commitment. It will influence most of the decisions you make thereafter. It's not a casual affair. This is self-examination.)

I want:
_____
_____
_____

Imagine achieving a result in your life that you deeply desire.

Example: Imagine you live where you most wish to live. Ignore how possible or impossible this vision seems. Imagine yourself accepting it into your life, the full manifestation of this result.

What is your ideal living environment:
_____
_____
_____

Describe in writing the experience you have imagined, using the present tense, as if it is happening now.

Where are you? _____

What does it look like? _____

How does it feel? _____

Describe it. _____
_____

Setting Goals   p. 195

Self-Image: *If you could become exactly the kind of person you wanted to be, what would your qualities be? How would you look, sound, act?*

_____

_____

Tangible: *What material things would you like to own?*

_____

_____

Health: *What's your desire for health, fitness, athletics, and anything to do with your body?*

_____

_____

Relationships: *What types of relationships would you like to have with 1. a partner, 2. friends, 3. family, 4. others?*

1. _____

2. _____

3. _____

4. _____

Work: *What is your ideal profession? What impact would you like your efforts to have?*

_____

_____

Personal Pursuits: *What would you like to create in the areas of individual learning, travel, reading, hobbies, avocation?*

_____

_____

Setting Goals   p. 196

Other: What other areas of life would you like to create?

___

Life Purpose: Imagine that your life has a unique purpose fulfilled through what you do. Describe that purpose.

___

STEP 2: Reflect on your first vision.

Did you articulate a vision that is close to what you actually want? There may be a variety of reasons why you found it hard to do.

> If you're now saying, "I can't have what I want," pretending you could have anything you want may not be an easy task.

In this exercise, you are trying to learn what your vision is. The question of whether it is possible is irrelevant.

For right now: Suspend your doubts, worries, fears, concerns about the limits of your future. Write as if real life could live up to your deepest wishes. What would happen then? Don't choose a vision based on what someone else wants.

A personal vision is not a done deal, already existing and waiting for you. It is something you create. This is your vision. If you're now saying, "I don't know what I want," write down your greatest wish/goal.

What is it?

___

A dream exists in you, even if you haven't put it into words. Your reluctance to articulate your vision is a sign of your not believing you can have what you want and a reluctance to take responsibility for your life. A goal is an expression of hope. Without hope, it is hard to make your dreams real.

STEP 3: Describe your personal Goal-Dream.

Imagine achieving the results in your life that you deeply desire.

Ask these questions – use the present tense as if it were happening right now. What would it look like? What words would you use to describe it?

Don't stop until a complete picture of what you want is there.

_____
_____
_____
_____

STEP 4: Expand and clarify your Vision-Goal-Dream.

Suspend judgment about what is "worth" desiring and ask instead:

> "Which aspects of these visions are closest to my deepest desires?"

Go back to your list and ask yourself the following questions:

1. If I could have it now, would I take it? Really?

_____
_____

Some elements of your dreams won't make it past this question. Accepting the responsibilities that go along with it. The ramifications.

> *Example:*
> Others pass the test conditionally, yes, but if...
> Others pass and are clarified in the process.
> You may be imprecise about your desires – even to you.

2. Assume you have it now – what does it bring you?

_____
_____

This question puts you into a richer image of your vision, so you can see its underlying implications more clearly. Why do you want it? What would it allow you to create? All responses are valid *if* they are your reasons.

Keep trying to understand what is important to you.

Setting Goals   p. 198

STEP 5: You may find that many components of your goal lead you to the same three or four primary goals.

You have a set of primary goals – sometimes they are buried so deeply it's not unusual for people to become emotional when they become aware of them. Keep asking the question, "What would it bring me?" This forces you to take the time to see what you deeply want.

Assignment: What do I want my life to look like?

Please buy large poster boards and colored magic markers. Using the new insights you have, create what you want your life to look like. Have fun with these – hang them up where you can view them, change them, add to them, keep them in mind. These are your dreams – your goals. Seeing them makes them real.

Years to Live:

My Goals:

Long Term: Year

_____
_____
_____
_____
_____
_____
_____

Short Term: Year

_____
_____
_____
_____
_____
_____
_____

                                                                                              Current Year

Section 8

Current Reality and Revising Goals

Your first vision is usually not your final one. As you work towards your dream, your understanding of what you want gradually grows more sophisticated. Inevitably, you reach some elements of your dream or reach other milestones that change your perception of what you care about.

This will help you "cycle back" to revisit your life's goals in light of <u>current reality</u>.

EXERCISE

Answer these ten questions for each of these aspects of your vision:

1. **Self Image** – What is my current self image? How has my vision changed for the kind of person I wish to be?

   _____
   _____

2. **Home** – Where do I live now? How has my vision changed for my living environment?

   _____
   _____

3. **Tangibles** – What is the real state of my tangible possessions? Vis-a-vis my vision? How has my vision changed for material possessions?

   _____
   _____

4. **Health** – What is the state of my health – fitness – anything else with my body?

   _____
   _____
   _____

Setting Goals   p. 200

5. **Relationships** – What is my current state in terms of personal relationships (primary), family, friends? How has my vision for relationships changed?

_____
_____
_____

6. **Work** – What is my professional situation? How has my job – career–related vision changed?

_____
_____
_____

7. **Pursuits** – What is my current reality regarding individual learning, hobbies, travel, reading, other activities? How has my vision changed?

_____
_____
_____

8. **Community** – What kind of community do I live in and belong to? How has my vision for community changed?

_____
_____
_____

9. **Other** – What are any other important aspects of current reality? How has my vision changed?

_____
_____
_____

10. **Life's Purpose** – What is current reality right now – in terms of my life's purpose, my goals? How have these as parts of my vision changed?

_____
_____
_____

Current Reality	**Desired Reality**
This is where you are.	This is where you want to go.
•	•

This causes **structural tension**, which is a discrepancy between how you currently live and your desired reality. All tension in life seeks resolution. This is a time you must be willing to do whatever it takes to get you the results you want.

The **creative process** starts by taking you from where you are to where you wish to be. There are lots of possibilities – are you willing to risk?

You'll be involved in the process of **intention**, which means developing an original path between your current reality and your goal. Once this process starts, momentum kicks in, and you will develop an instinct for finding the most effective actions that will lead you to your goal. It's a time to stay focused and put all your energies into your dream.

- Impose deadlines on yourself — keep on track.
- There may be times you slow down — this happens — you are human.
- There may be roadblocks that don't let you see your goal. Don't let these discourage you. Keep going.

Assignment:

Earlier, I asked you to create (on a large poster board) what you wanted your life to look like. I now want you to do a similar exercise, however, this time set it up with the headings of "My Current Reality" and "My Desired Reality."

Get *tough* on yourself:

Start canceling useless activities in your life.

EXERCISE

What do I waste time doing?

_____
_____
_____
_____

MY Goal Experience

Ask yourself frequently:

> "Is what I am doing right now helping me reach my goals?"

If the answer is no, stop what you're doing.

The choice is yours:

You will limit your progress (doing insignificant activities).

So please concentrate on significant activities that keep you on track, and help you reach your goals!

The key is:

Do not minor in majors
Do not major in minors
MAJOR IN MAJORS

These are important activities which will propel you towards your goals.

Your personal success plan should include:

1. **Crystal-Clear Thinking**

   A. Sit – Think – Determine what specific goal or goals you will achieve.

   B. Consciously dedicate yourself to the attainment of these goals.

   C. Have an unswerving purpose.

   D. Go after the goals with zeal.

   E. Keep focused.

2. **Develop a plan of action for achieving these goals**

   A. Set a deadline to reach these goals.

   B. Carefully track your progress. (Start with baby steps, if needed.)
   Hour by hour, day in and day out, week by week, month by month.
   Organized activities will propel you towards reaching them.

   C. Your enthusiasm towards reaching your desired goals will give you the power to reach them.
   Remember: Rome wasn't built in a day.

3. **The sincere desire for the reaching of these goals is essential**

   A. Your desire for successfully reaching your goal implants "success consciousness" which is fed to your subconscious mind. This starts the "Success Habit." If you're not in it to win, you're not in it.

   B. Your inner burning desire will be a great motivator of actions you must take to reach your goals.

Setting Goals   p. 204

Section 9

Making Things Happen

**What is your objective? Your target?
The result is the <u>goal</u> you wish to achieve.**

Reasons many fail:

- low motivation
- unclear objectives
- poorly formed action plans
- failure to stay focused

TO SUCCEED, LET'S GO!

No. 1 – Clarifying your objectives/goals. Let's work on three.
Goal 1 _____
Goal 2 _____
Goal 3 _____

No. 2 – Identifying the proper steps

An objective is <u>a desired outcome</u>, <u>a target</u>, <u>a result</u>, a "<u>goal</u>" you wish to achieve. Objectives give you a sense of direction. Objectives help you define what you want.

There are 11 steps toward clear objectives:

1. State your objective clearly.
2. Ask yourself why you want what you want.
3. State clearly how you will know when your objective has been met (this ensures clarity). How will you indentify it? What will it look like, feel like?
4. Make your objective specific.
5. State when you want to reach your goal and why.
6. Be clear for whom you want this.
7. Check to see if any of your objectives conflict; if so, which is a priority?
8. Identify any constraints (external/internal) that will make this difficult.
9. Identify your resources that should help you succeed.
10. Check that your objective is realistic.
11. Know what obstacles you may run into.

Setting Goals   p. 205

HOW DO YOU FEEL NOW THAT YOU SEE YOUR GOAL IN BLACK & WHITE?

NOW YOU HAVE CLEARLY DEFINED GOALS.

EXERCISE

Identifying Positive/Negative Forces

IN ALL CHANGES: There will be positive forces which will assist you. There will be negative forces which will work against you. So, let's identify which forces in your life will be helpful and which forces will work against you.

Examples: Working for you: Working against you:

- I'm young
- I'm bright
- I have high energy

- I don't have a college degree
- I don't wish to relocate
- I'm very disorganized

Goal 1:_____   Goal 2: _____   Goal 3: _____

↓ **Forces working for the change:**

    Goal 1   Goal 2   2Goal 3

_____
_____
_____
_____
_____
_____
_____
_____
_____
_____
_____
_____
_____
_____

↑ **Forces working against the change.**

Setting Goals   p. 206

1. Identifying Your Goal
- Deal with one goal at a time
- Be very specific
- Date you wish to achieve goal

2. List Forces Working for You
- A positive force is anything that will contribute to you achieving your goal
- Who? What? Where? When? How Much? How Many?

3. List Forces Working against You
- There are negative forces you must overcome
- Who? What? Where? When? How much? How many?
- Be specific
- List all factors: Internal/External

4. Analyze the Forces
- These forces should be real, not assumed
- Things that have a significant effect on whether you reach your goal or not

5. Start to Strengthen the Positive – Weaken the Negative
- After identifying which forces are most important, work on each important force in turn
- Identify ways to minimize each force working against you
- Identify any you really cannot eliminate – write "no action possible"

(Don't use this step as a cop-out for difficult but workable situations.)

- Identify ways to increase – strengthen – maximize each positive force

6. Assess How Feasible Your Objective Action Plan Seems to Be
- *Ask yourself:* Do the positives clearly outweigh the negatives, or will they when I have maximized and minimized them?

Setting Goals   p. 207

- If *YES* is the answer:
    Question to ask yourself: "Do I really want to achieve this?"
    - If the answer is *NO*, your choice is to abandon it or change/modify the original idea by reducing your sights or revising the target date

7. **Don't Be Trapped by Your Opinion of How to Reach Your Goal!**
    - This is a time to be open to all possibilities
    - It's imperative that you keep an open mind

Section 10

The Big Picture

The World is a Big Dream Machine...
Learn How to Access It.

Think about the Big Picture. Your plan should include all of your dreams and goals.

In order for you to be successful, you must put your life plan in to a

<u>"real timeframe."</u>

You have no way of knowing what you'll really be doing or wanting in five years or ultimately. Many things will come into play – chance, love, luck, loss, health, political and economic forces, etc., which you'll have no control over.

However, having a "<u>sketch</u>" of what you want your future to look like serves two purposes:

- It nudges you to meet your deadlines.
- It alerts you to all the possibilities open to you. It's a smart idea to jot them down as considerations.

As you progress towards your current goals,

future dreams start to look real and possible.

You start to understand from your experience that

YOU REALLY DO SHAPE YOUR DESTINY!

YOU HAVE THE POWER!

Setting Goals   p. 209

GOALS Must be
S – M – A – R – T

Specific   (crystal clear)

Ex: I will find a house with at least 1-1/2 acres with a stone wall in the front and an attached garage. There will be a fireplace in the kitchen…(when you see it or produce it, it's identifiable).

Measurable   (you know what the results will look like)

Ex: I want $1,000 in five savings accounts by December 15. looking at the savings books, there would be stamped $1,000.00 with dates before December 15.

Attainable   (within the realm of possibilities)

Ex: I wish to lose 10 lbs. in 6 months. This is attainable. To say I will lose 50 lbs. in a month is not.

Realistic   (don't beat yourself up by setting a goal you can't reach)

Ex: Deciding to run the Boston Marathon when you are 9 months pregnant and have never trained, unrealistic. Deciding to train for the Marathon 18 months in advance of the actual April 19th date by putting together a training program, this is realistic.

Timely   (there is a time for everything)

Ex: A goal to find a field of daisies to photograph in January in New England is not timely. To photograph a snow scene in January in New England is timely.

Section 11

Your Personal Goal-Setting Plan

Please answer the following questions and, this time, be very specific. THIS IS A SERIOUS EXERCISE, AND IT MUST BE DONE IN WRITING.

EXERCISE

MY Specific Goals

1. What is your ULTIMATE GOAL? Whatever your dream is, write it down. Don't forget to put down a specific attainment date.

ULTIMATE GOAL:

Attainment Date:

2. What do you want to accomplish in your life, in the next two to three years? List all of these. Choose three goals which you want most. Give each a completion date. These are your LONG-TERM GOALS.

LONG-TERM GOAL:

Attainment Date:

LONG-TERM GOAL:

Attainment Date:

LONG-TERM GOAL:

Attainment Date:

Setting Goals   p. 211

3. List all the things you want to become, you want to do, and you want to have within the next year. Write them down under the heading, ONE-YEAR GOALS. Give each a specific completion date.

ONE-YEAR GOAL:
_____
_____

Attainment Date:
_____

ONE-YEAR GOAL:
_____
_____

Attainment Date:
_____

ONE-YEAR GOAL:
_____
_____

Attainment Date:
_____

4. 90-DAY GOALS: What can you do in the next 90 days that will help you to accomplish your one-year goals? What skills do you need to develop? What weaknesses do you have to correct? What experiences can give you the competitive edge? Write all these down.
_____
_____
_____

5. What can you do TODAY that will lead you one step closer to your 90-day goals? Write it down.

TODAY I WILL:
_____
_____
_____
_____
_____

Setting Goals   p. 212

FOLLOW-THROUGH

In order for you to turn your dreams into reality, you must take actions. (I understand even a small step is a start.)

EXERCISE

I will start working on my three top priorities:

#1 Goal: _____

Action Steps I will take:
_____
_____
_____
_____

#2 Goal: _____

Action Steps I will take:
_____
_____
_____
_____

#3 Goal: _____

Action Steps I will take:
_____
_____
_____
_____
_____

MY Action Steps

Section 12

Your Planning Wall

I highly recommend that you create a series of charts that will map your plan of action in all areas, month-by-month, week-by-week, day-by-day, and hang them on a wall.

You will need to purchase some items for this important project:

1. Cork board (cut out photos – tack up anything you wish to have in your life)

2. Create a flow chart – which I will explain in the next section

3. Goals Calendar
   – Short term: 3 mo., 6 mo., 1 year
   – Long term: 2 years, 5 years
   – Ultimate Goals

4. monthly calendar
   – One-year plans, 2-year, 5-year
   – Life Plan: All your dreams and goals of your life. (I understand I can change these; they are my goals.)

5. Weekly calendar

6. Daily planner

7. Master list

8. List of immediate priority steps: 1st steps

9. Time log – 6am to 6pm (time used, time you can clear to start working on your goals)

10. Pocket appointment book

Setting Goals   p. 214

Planning Wall

Your planning wall is your *conscience*, your *guide*, your *boss*, your *security blanket*.

Make it attractive, colorful, and easy for you to work with.

Keep it updated. It shows you how you're doing.

In front of you, it shows you:

1. What you must do this week
2. What you must do today
3. What you must do tomorrow

Check off completed work.

Chart your progress.

AND Reward yourself!

Your Goal Calendar maps your flow chart onto time, giving you a tentative schedule against which you can check your pace and progress.

Your Goal Calendar gives you the actual timing, accounting for reality factors – like Christmas rush, summer vacation, deadlines on applications – just how long things are likely to take. Your Goal Calendar lets you know which of those first steps you "should" start doing tomorrow.

When you've completed your calendar, you will have your goals planted firmly in "Real Time." You've defined your first steps – clear-cut, short-term tasks with fairly pressing deadlines. Now focus on these – forget what's further down the line. You've entrusted it all to paper – it's there, it's real, it won't go away. You'll know if you're on schedule – just look ahead at the next deadline on your calendar.

Any time you need to be reminded why you're doing what you're doing, just glance at your flow chart and see exactly where today's Action Steps fit into the context of your plan.

Scheduling Your First Steps:

Your Goal Calendar makes it clear which of these first steps must be taken immediately – a priority, and which can wait.

List of Immediate Priority Steps:

Put these on your planning wall. Start scheduling them one-by-one into the days of the week. Once you get into action, each week is going to be a whole new ball game.

Be sure there is a TONIGHT REVIEW/TOMORROW pad on your planning wall.

CAUTION

In any journey, you can take either a direct or indirect route. This is true in goal setting.

Ask yourself these questions:

- Am I doing the best thing right now to assure my reaching my goals? If the answer is no, stop.
- Does accomplishing my daily goals take me one step closer to my 90-day goals?
- Do my 90-day goals lead me to my one-year and long-term goals?
- Will this route eventually bring me to my ultimate goal?
- Am I on the most direct route?

Take one step at a time, **but first make sure that you are headed in the right direction. If not, make corrections!**

STAY AWAKE • PAY ATTENTION • STAY FOCUSED

Your Flow Chart
(Right in the center of your planning wall)
It's the master plan that coordinates everything.
More than one goal, put up a flow chart for each goal (different colors).

Your flow chart gives you the logic of the plan. It works each branch of action down to first steps.

You may have to adjust your target date. You can't know in advance how long some things will take. Things can come up that are not predictable – some will help you along, some will set you back. Target Date: Set a date – it shows serious intent. A deadline – it helps you get yourself in gear.

Goal Calendar

Start

JAN
FEB
MAR
APR
MAY
JUNE

Target Date

1. Look at major steps on Flow Chart.

2. If you don't have clearly defined goals, set some.

3. You need checkpoints to regulate the pace of your progress.

4. Assign each step a target date (write it down). This eliminates panic and rewards you with a frequent, rechargeable sense of accomplishment.

Section 13

Become a Goal Setter

Stop letting life "happen to you"

Every successful business has a business plan. Take a lesson from that and put together your own "Business Plan for Life."

Successful people operate from goals.

Without goals, you are on a trip without a destination.

Without goals, you will drift and not accomplish your dreams.

Goals are results we are committed to producing – if it is a goal, it means you are going to take action.

"Do the thing and you will have the power," said Emerson.

Remember:

They are your goals.

You can change them if they become inappropriate!

Setting Goals   p. 218

Helpful Forms for your goal-setting

Make copies and fill in appropriate time frames.

Ex: **Short-term**   **Long-term**

3 months

_____

6 months

_____

1 year

_____

2 years

_____

5 years

_____

Short-Term:

_____
_____
_____

Long-Term:

_____
_____
_____

EXERCISE

MY Goals

Desired Goal: _____

Target Date: _____

Benefits to be Enjoyed:
_____
_____
_____

Obstacles and Roadblocks:
1. _____
2. _____
3. _____

Solutions and Plans: *Completion Date:*

1. a. _____
    b. _____
    c. _____
2. a. _____
    b. _____
    c. _____
3. a. _____
    b. _____
    c. _____

DAILY: AM I MOVING TOWARD MY GOAL?
_____
_____

Setting Goals   p. 220

EXERCISE

A Goal for MY Success

GOAL
_____

OVERALL TARGET DATE – *I will reach my goal on or before:*
_____

OBSTACLES AND ROADBLOCKS – *These stand between me and my goals:*
_____

SOLUTIONS AND PLANS – *I will overcome obstacles by taking these actions:*
_____
_____

EXPECTED BENEFITS – *Reaching this goal will benefit me in these ways:*
_____

IS IT WORTH IT TO ME? – *Am I willing to invest the time and effort to obtain the expected benefits?* _____ YES _____ NO
_____

PROGRESS REPORT – *My progress rating on the date indicated:*

Date _____ Poor _____ Fair _____ Good _____ Excellent _____

Date _____ Poor _____ Fair _____ Good _____ Excellent _____

Date _____ Poor _____ Fair _____ Good _____ Excellent _____

Date _____ Poor _____ Fair _____ Good _____ Excellent _____

Setting Goals   p. 221

Section 14

Scared Free

The section you are just finishing on goal-setting is key to your success.

In America at age 65:

> 55% of the population will be broke
>
> 42% will be okay, counting heavily on Social Security, but will need supplementary income, need to depend on children
>
> 3% will be independently wealthy

If this isn't a wake-up call, I don't know what is. What group do you want to be in?

I called this scared free because it scared me into action. After hearing this statistic at a seminar I attended at age 40, it freed me from old belief systems, old patterns and old behavior. It made me look at what my life looked like at that point and what I needed to do to "Wake-Up" - "Get Unstuck" and end up in the 3% of independently wealthy people.

Setting Goals   p. 222

Chapter 5 Review Page - Setting Goals

Setting Goals   p. 224

Setting Goals   p. 225

CHAPTER 6

"Tanny's Strategies for Success"

CHAPTER 6 – TABLE OF CONTENTS

Section		Page
1	How to Get What You Want!	230
	Exercise: I'm Willing to Take Control	231
2	Trade-Offs	232
	Exercise: MY Past Trade-Offs	232
	Exercise: Trade-Offs I Face Now	233
3	Mind Mapping	234
	Exercise: Making a Mind Map	235
	Exercise: MY Mind Map	237
4	Time Management	238
	Exercise: MY Time Is Money	239
	Exercise: MY Daily Time Use	241
	Exercise: Analyzing MY Habits of Time Use	242
	Exercise: MY Plan of Action for Change	243
5	Why Bother to Plan?	244
6	How to Plan	246
	Exercise: MY Yearly Tasks	248
	Exercise: Planning for a Goal	249
	Exercise: Planning for an Activity	250
	Exercise: MY Monthly Tasks	251
	Exercise: MY Weekly Tasks	253
7	How to Do a "TO-DO" List	254
	Exercise: MY Daily TO-DO List	256
8	Practical Hints for Planning	257

Section 1

How to Get What You Want!

To get what you want, you must take the responsibility that whatever your life looks like right now, you have caused it to be that way; your health, finances, relationships, professional life, etc.

Consciously or subconsciously, you have invented yourself. And you can

RE-INVENT YOURSELF!

Once you realize that you make the choices that determine the quality of your life, a powerful force within yourself will help you create the future you want. Understanding your are in control puts you in the driver's seat (a place you've been all along without realizing it!). Once you accept responsibility for creating your life up to now, you are READY to assume responsibility for having it become exactly what you want.

ARE YOU WILLING TO TAKE CONTROL?

"WILLINGNESS" IS THE KEY.
IT'S THE *ONLY* KEY...AND YOU OWN IT.

"Willingness" has great <u>power</u>. <u>Willingness</u> is a <u>frame of mind</u> which is open to every possible request made of you. Judging, having reservations or refusing to trust any of these will cause you to not get what you want.

When it comes to "getting the results you wish," intention is as important as action. <u>Intention</u> is a non-action which is just as capable of producing tangible results as an action step may be. People with strong intentions are hard to stop. Become one of these people.

Strategy for Success   p. 230

To get what you want from life is as easy as **A-B-C**:

  A. Accept responsibility for creating the way your world looks right now.

  B. Be responsible for any change (intention) you deserve.

  C. Control your own future by putting yourself in charge.

These three steps do not require any physical actions on your part. They are "Shifts in Attitude."

This may be a new approach to your life:
Understanding I am the cause of what happens in my life from now on.

EXERCISE

What am I ready to take responsibility for right now in my life?

I'm Willing to Take Control

Strategy for Success   p. 231

Section 2

Trade-Offs

Many things in life are trade-offs. We are making trade-offs constantly in our lives.

A few examples of trade-offs would be:

1. If you wish to be a runway model, you can't indulge in gourmet food and rich, buttery desserts every day.
2. If you choose to live in Kansas, you can't walk out your front door and dive into the ocean.
3. If you choose to spend all your money on trips, you won't have a large savings account.

EXERCISE

MY Past Trade-Offs

Relationships? Career? Habits? People? Ideas?
1) _____
2) _____
3) _____

Relationships? Career? Habits? People? Ideas?
1) _____
2) _____

How we make trade-offs determines the quality of our life.

Success depends in a large measure on making effective trade-offs. Trade-offs always involve the experience of loss. You must give up something to get something else. You must be clear on what it is costing you and be willing to accept the price. The costs can be physical, mental, etc.

Strategy for Success   p. 232

Famous saying:

"Life can only be understood backwards, but it must be lived forward."

You and I proceed at best with educated guesses about optimal <u>trade-offs</u> for ourselves.

EXERCISE

What trade-offs are you facing in your life right now?

Trade-Offs I Face Now

1. _____
2. _____
3. _____
4. _____
5. _____

Strategy for Success   p. 233

Section 3

Mind Mapping

"Writing down ideas gets your mind unstuck."

Mind mapping is a technique of mapping on paper – quite literally – the thoughts of your mind. It's a non-linear technique that uses both sides of your brain. It allows you to capture thoughts fast and efficiently. It was developed by a leading brain researcher, Tony Buzan.

Suggestions for use include:

      problem solving   leisure/pleasure
      time management   financial planning
      personal goals   brainstorming
      educating children   business planning

Mind mapping can be used for a quick first pass at developing a sophisticated plan.

Mind mapping is a very creative technique. It starts the creative juices flowing. It's quick, so you do not lose ideas. It saves time and is effective and efficient.

Mind mapping uses the untapped potential of

Your Brain

3 lbs. of gray matter

10 - 15 billion nerve cells capable of making 10,000 connections

Your brain has the capability of storing more information than all the libraries in the world!

Strategy for Success   p. 234

The brain is being analyzed constantly. The unique interactions which comprise the mind remain a mystery. The brain is very complex. Everything you see, hear, taste, touch, every emotion, motion, every thought happens because of your brain. You'll be using the untapped potential in your brain to do mind-mapping exercises.

EXERCISE

Making a Mind Map

How to do a Mind Map:

1. Draw a circle in the middle of the page. Write the title of your project in the middle. Include pictures or symbols.

2. Next, draw lines out from the circle similar to spokes of a wheel (each reflects a key area or action needed). As you map these items, you will think of items related to them. Radiate these out from under the spoke they are related to.

Add additional areas as you think of them. Keep the items on your mind map general. It is not an "items to do" list.

A mind map is a visual picture of the main areas that need your attention.

3. Then: List your key activities. Using your mind map as a reference, list all of the action items you will need to do to complete this picture. Make clear directives, starting with an action word. After you have listed all the key activities for this project, put a DUE DATE after each one. This time line gives you the chronological order in which the activities have to be completed. Next, look at each activity and estimate the amount of time it will take to complete. Some will take five minutes, some hours, others months.

Creative planning uses both sides of the brain and encourages imaginative thinking.

Doing a mind map for projects gives you the opportunity to be creative, **"right brained"** in your planning, which is normally a left brain function. They are a creative, simple, non-linear way of recording information.

The PRIMARY TOOLS you'll be using are:

Your Mind

It will give you a deep appreciation of the power of your mind. It will broaden your perspective, and you will become a better thinker.

Your Imagination

Your imagination is powerful. Learn to have fun with it. Enjoy yourself and go with what it's presenting to you. You will be amazed at what you will come up with.

Your Creativity

Using mind maps unlocks your creativity. It allows us to look at options. It helps us move past mental barriers. The biggest barrier is the voice in your head which constantly tells you why something won't work. Stop listening!

Strategy for Success   p. 235

HOW DO YOU DO IT?
- Don't judge – just write!
- Allow ideas to flow freely.
- Key words are used to represent ideas.
- One key word per line.
- Key word ideas are connected to the central focus with lines.
- Color is used to highlight/emphasize ideas.
- Images/symbols are used to highlight ideas – stimulate the mind to make other connections.

Here's an example of how it will look:

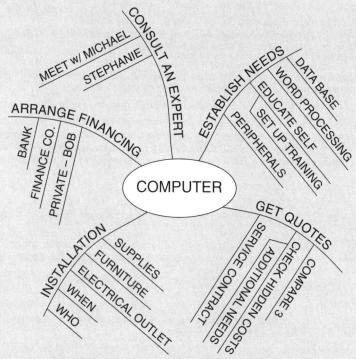

Mind mapping allows you to quickly get ideas down in key word form.
- It allows you to quickly make connections and associations.
- It allows you to quickly add your thoughts, ideas, feelings.

Mind mapping is not an end result – it's a process.

Whatever you do on your mind map is okay.

There are no wrong mind maps.

Strategy for Success   p. 236

EXERCISE

Create your own mind map for an area that needs your attention.

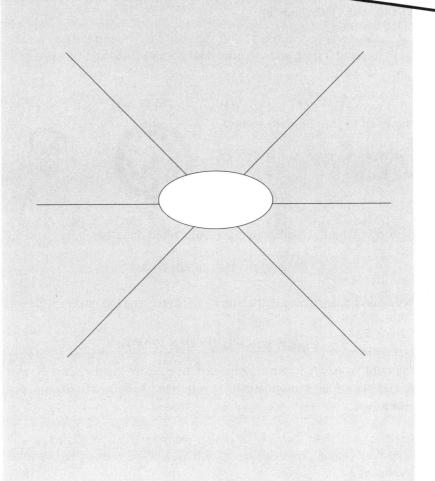

Strategy for Success   p. 237

Section 4

Time Management

Imagine you had a bank that each morning credited your account with $1,440, with ONE condition:

> Whatever part of the $1,440 you didn't use during the day would be erased from your account, and no balance would be carried forward.

What would you do? I bet you'd draw out EVERY RED CENT, EVERY DAY, and use it to your best advantage.

Well, YOU DO HAVE SUCH A BANK, and its name is

TIME!

Every morning, this bank credits you with 1,440 minutes.

HOW DO YOU SPEND THEM?

How you choose to "use it or abuse it" will determine the quality of life you will lead.

HOW MUCH IS MY TIME WORTH?

You must know what your time is worth to evaluate the time cost of what you do. It's valuable information! Do you spend $5.00 worth of time on a 5-cent job?

The following chart shows what time is worth by the hour, based on 244 eight-hour working days per year (assuming a five-day week, less vacation and holidays).

Strategy for Success   p. 238

If Your Annual Earnings are:	Every Hour is Worth:
$ 10,000	$ 5.12
12,000	6.15
15,000	7.68
18,000	9.22
20,000	10.25
25,000	12.81
30,000	15.37
35,000	17.93
40,000	20.49
50,000	25.61
60,000	30.74
75,000	38.42
100,000	51.23

Time is important – Time is money.

EXERCISE

Some things you do are more important and more profitable than other things. Below, list the six most important things you do, in descending order (with number one being the most valuable and profitable). From now on, spend as much time as possible on the important, profitable activities you have defined here.

1) _____
2) _____
3) _____
4. _____
5. _____
6. _____

MY Time Is Money

How you use your valuable time is up to yu…

Don't abdicate the right to your time!

Strategy for Success   p. 239

Let's now look at the two primary factors behind the choices we make on how to use our time:

URGENCY & IMPORTANCE

KNOWING WHAT IS IMPORTANT instead of simply responding to what is urgent is the FIRST STEP to putting FIRST THINGS FIRST.

How much does urgency affect our choices? Deadlines at work, family members, the phone.

We are so used to the adrenaline rush of handling crises that we start to depend on getting energy from the feeling of excitement. How does urgency feel? Stressful, pressured, tense, exhausting – yes, but it can also be exhilarating. We feel useful, successful, up to the task. We feel validated. We get a temporary "high" from solving urgent and important problems. Then when the importance isn't there, the urgency fix is so powerful that we are drawn to do anything urgent just to keep moving.

Urgency is an addiction – a very self-destructive behavior. When urgency is the dominant factor in our lives, it overrides things that are merely important. Urgent things become "first things." We get so caught up in a whirlwind of activity that we don't stop to ask if what we're doing really needs to be done.

MANY IMPORTANT THINGS – THOSE THAT LEAD US TO OUR OBJECTIVES AND GIVE MEANING TO OUR LIVES – DON'T DEMAND OUR IMMEDIATE ATTENTION! Because they ARE NOT "URGENT," THEY ARE PRECISELY THE THINGS THAT WE MUST ACT UPON.

How can we keep both our focus and a larger perspective? The answer is a planning technique that links the big picture with the immediate needs of the day in a balanced, realistic way.

Begin each day with the end results you want in mind.

Do the things that will propel you to where you want to be.

Prioritize your schedule.

Schedule your priorities.

Strategy for Success   p. 240

EXERCISE

MY Daily Time Use

PERSONAL   Date: _____

Time	How I spent my time	Minutes wasted and why
6:00 a.m.		
7:00 a.m.		
8:00 a.m.		
9:00 a.m.		
10:00 a.m.		
11:00 a.m.		
12:00 noon		
1:00 p.m.		
2:00 p.m.		
3:00 p.m.		
4:00 p.m.		
5:00 p.m.		
6:00 p.m.		
7:00 p.m.		
8:00 p.m.		
9:00 p.m.		
10:00 p.m.		
11:00 p.m.		

Total time wasted: _____

PROFESSIONAL   Date: _____

Time	How I spent my time	Minutes wasted and why
6:00 a.m.		
7:00 a.m.		
8:00 a.m.		
9:00 a.m.		
10:00 a.m.		
11:00 a.m.		
12:00 noon		
1:00 p.m.		
2:00 p.m.		
3:00 p.m.		
4:00 p.m.		
5:00 p.m.		
6:00 p.m.		
7:00 p.m.		
8:00 p.m.		
9:00 p.m.		
10:00 p.m.		
11:00 p.m.		

Total time wasted _____

Strategy for Success   p. 241

EXERCISE

Analyzing MY Habits of Time Use

PERSONAL

My inappropriate time behaviors	How I feel when I act this way	How I would like to act	Benefits I would get from changing my behavior

WORK

My inappropriate time behaviors at work	How I feel when I act this way	How I would like to act	Benefits I would get from changing my behavior at work

Strategy for Success   p. 242

EXERCISE

Actions which will increase time spent with high-payoff activities:

WORK

TASKS	ACTION I WILL TAKE

WORK

TASKS	ACTION I WILL TAKE

Strategy for Success   p. 243

Section 5

Why Bother to Plan?

Planning means decision making, being organized. In life, we are constantly making decisions. Ninety percent (90%) of these decisions recur. If we make them once, we'll make them a thousand times. Deciding what to have for dinner is a typical recurring decision. When to do your laundry is another.

The other ten percent (10%) of these decisions do not recur. They occur only a few times in a lifetime. These are called "critical decisions." Deciding to get married or to move are examples of critical decisions. Most critical decisions requires time, thought, knowledge, and risk. The decision-maker must think before making critical decisions. Some critical decisions must be made quickly. These involve life-threatening situations.

Critical decisions take time and should be taken seriously. <u>Planning</u> helps you concentrate fully and completely on these critical decisions which have a major impact on your future. Planning should be part of the process. Planning relieves you of the minor, recurring decisions. For example, you decide that every Saturday, you will wash your car. You'll never have to make that decision again. <u>By planning each and every recurring decision, you clear your mind and focus on important decisions you face</u>. You have more time now to think about critical decisions, such as buying a summer home or looking for a new career.

Taking the time to plan and make decisions once and for all about minor details, you free yourself from worry, guilt, frustration and anxiety. You now feel a sense of control. You start to major in major life challenges – and not minor in majors. You will know where you spend your time and find your productivity will increase.

To start what you wish to accomplish, you must list all details requiring decisions, such as when to wash the car and when you're going to write the third chapter of your book. Next, you schedule these details, making a

Strategy for Success   p. 244

decision about them once – and stick to it. Every Saturday, you wash your car. You spend three hours a day writing. Now you don't have to think about it again.

First, planning takes care of both details and activities (tasks you perform towards the achievement of your goals). Once you have programmed your week with a workable mix of essential details (washing the car) and activities (writing three chapters in your book), you are free to get going and do them! It's simply a question of figuring out what you want to accomplish and when.

That's what planning is.

Once you have planned your activities and goals, <u>you have freed yourself to do them</u>. You no longer need to remember something or try to squeeze something in. The part I love most about planning is it frees you up to think creatively. <u>With a free mind, your thought process becomes clear</u>.

You can focus on important goals. Reach your goals.

In the next section, I will show you how to create a workable plan.

Section 6

How to Plan

Choose a time (allow yourself two hours).

- You may use your computer or notebook and pen.
- Have your last year's and this year's calendar.

You're set to begin:

1. Make a list of your yearly tasks:

- OPTIONAL, such as planting flowers
- MUST DO, such as paying taxes

Take each goal separately and break it down into activities. Decide which activities you will complete this year. See the exercises on pages 249 and 250.

List all tasks that recur monthly. *Ex:* balancing your bank statement

List all tasks that recur weekly. *Ex:* grocery shopping

2. Make a decision about each optional task:

A. Schedule the completion of yearly optional tasks at your convenience. For example, plan to plant your garden during the first week of May. In addition, plan the completion of those must do tasks that must be done. For example, plan to finish your income tax work by April 1.

B. Break down your goals into activities and also choose which activities you will do this year. Next, take each activity and plan how much time it will take weekly. For example, if my goal is learning to play tennis, one activity could be practicing two hours three days a week.

Strategy for Success   p. 246

C. Design both weekly and monthly forms. Take each form and decide when you want to do the weekly and monthly recurring tasks. Schedule them accordingly and write them down.

3. Planning:

A. Once a year, transfer all yearly information to a new year calendar. Make appropriate additions and deletions.

B. Once a month, look at the year calendar and your monthly schedule. Add the particular duties of the new month (taken from the year calendar) to the monthly schedule. For example, in September, you will schedule a recurring task such as closing off your summer cottage and putting your storm windows on.

C. Once a week, look at your calendar and your weekly schedule. Write a new schedule for the following week, including: any monthly task that falls due that week; all recurring weekly activities, such as filling the car up; and any necessary tasks, such as a dentist appointment.

D. Make a TO-DO list every day! I'll give you plenty of hints on TO-DO lists after the following exercises.

EXERCISE

MY Yearly Tasks

	MUST DO		*OPTIONAL*
Month	Task	Frequency	Task
JAN			
FEB			
MAR			
APR			
MAY			
JUN			
JUL			
AUG			
SEP			
OCT			
NOV			
DEC			

Strategy for Success   p. 248

EXERCISE

Planning for a Goal

GOAL: _____

Completion Date: _____

Activities (in logical order):

1. _____
2. _____
3. _____
4. _____
5. _____
6. _____

Resources for each activity:

1. _____
_____
2. _____
_____
3. _____
_____
4. _____
_____
5. _____
_____
6. _____
_____

This year's activities: Due Date

1. _____
2. _____
3. _____

Strategy for Success   p. 249

EXERCISE

Planning for an Activity

GOAL: _____
Completion: _____
Activity: _____

Steps to complete activity: Due date:

1. _____
2. _____
3. _____
5. _____
5. _____
6. _____
7. _____
8. _____
9. _____
10. _____

Resources:

1. _____
2. _____
3. _____
4. _____
5. _____
6. _____

Activity that precedes this one:
_____
_____

Activity that succeeds this one:
_____
_____

Strategy for Success   p. 250

EXERCISE

MY Monthly Tasks

Week One:
1. _____
2. _____
3. _____
4. _____
5. _____
6. _____
7. _____

Week Two:
8. _____
9. _____
10. _____
11. _____
12. _____
13. _____
14. _____

Week Three:
15. _____
16. _____
17. _____
18. _____
19. _____
20. _____
21. _____

Week Four:
22. _____
23. _____
24. _____
25. _____
26. _____
27. _____
28. _____

Week Five:
29. _____
30. _____
31. _____

Additional:

Strategy for Success   p. 251

EXERCISE

MY Monthly Tasks

TIME			
MONDAY			
TUESDAY			
WEDNESDAY			
THURSDAY			
FRIDAY			
WEEKENDS			

Strategy for Success   p. 252

EXERCISE

MY Weekly Tasks

MONDAY: _____
TUESDAY: _____
WEDNESDAY: _____
THURSDAY: _____
FRIDAY: _____
WEEKEND: _____

MONDAY
AM
PM

TUESDAY
AM
PM

WEDNESDAY
AM
PM

THURSDAY
AM
PM

FRIDAY
AM
PM

WEEKEND
AM
PM

Strategy for Success p. 253

Section 7

How to Do a "TO-DO" List

What is a TO-DO list?

The list consists of a combination of duties (such as washing your car) and activities (such as writing chapters in your book). A duty is a task necessary to survive. An activity is a someting you do that brings you closer to your goals. Most people share similar duties, but our activities are very different. Include in each day something that brings you enjoyment.

Why make a TO-DO list?

Planning TO-DO lists enables you to make the best use of your time <u>at all times</u>. Planning alleviates the frustration you feel when you put unrealistic expectations on yourself.

Making your TO-DO list:

Not included in this list are obvious responsibilities such as going to work, personal hygiene, etc. Each morning or before bed, make a list of all the duties and activities that you want to accomplish for the day. Limit yourself to 8 items! Make those 8 items an even mixture of activities and duties. No more than 8 – don't set yourself up to fail. It works best for me to do my TO-DO list before I go to bed. Once I write down what I wish to accomplish the next day, I feel more in control.

Decide on your day's priorities. Put an ✶ next to must do's.

Example of my day:	S.N.I. meeting 7 a.m. - 11 a.m.
	Phone Brent
	Pick up mail from P.O. box
	Doctor's appointment at 3 PM ✶
	Have dinner with Ellen
	Work on Chapter 6 of my book
	Write to Jon, Ann and Veronica
	Phone follow up

Strategy for Success   p. 254

Peak Energy:

Know your high- and low-energy levels during a 24-hour period and schedule accordingly. The most important and difficult (i.e., top priority) should be done when you are at your peak. This will give you the best chance of succeeding. Do low-priority items last and when your energy level is not as high. I know my energy is best in the morning, so I plan my day accordingly.

Take time to relax:

Schedule time for yourself every day for nothing but relaxing. You must restore yourself, recharge your batteries. Do something you enjoy.

Cross off the finished items. Move the unfinished to tomorrow's list – do not indefinitely move unfinished items to a new list! Give yourself only three days to do them. If something is still unfinished at the end of the third day, consider someone else doing it for you if it must be done. If you have to do it, do it the next day. Don't let unfinished work sit on lists indefinitely.

A word of <u>CAUTION</u>!

Be flexible in making your TO-DO list. When you plan your time, allow for emergencies and unexpected happenings. Remember, it's a tool you use to get organized that helps you reach your goals.

When you miss working on a top-priority activity, don't worry about it. Never try to catch up by doing twice as much the next day. Just keep up a steady pace: missing a day or two won't matter in the big picture.

It's easy to be distracted from important, difficult projects. You can't always clear the decks before beginning a project. You may never get around to top-priority projects. You'll find yourself too tired, without the energy you need for an A activity.

EXERCISE

MY Daily TO-DO List

Priority: Description:

Notes/Ideas:

Strategy for Success   p. 256

Section 8

Practical Hints for Planning

Planning is the best tool you can use to achieve your goals. A conscious decision about how to spend your time (time management) through planning eliminates anxiety, frustration and puts you in

CONTROL!

Please keep the following in mind as you plan your time:

1. All plans must be subject to change. Things change, so stay flexible. It's unrealistic to think you need only one plan for a lifetime. Your plans will need revisions
2. Make planning easier with the right equipment and supplies.
3. Do not use planning to procrastinate. Plan and do it!
4. Track your progress and reward yourself.
5. Remember: You are a human being, not a machine. We all make mistakes and fail. Planning is a tool. Do not overload yourself. When you do fail, give yourself a break and move forward.
6. Make certain that you make time for yourself every single day. Not to do this is cheating yourself.

Strategy for Success   p. 257

Chapter 6 Review Page - Tanny's Strategy for Success

Strategy for Success   p. 258

Strategy for Success p. 259

CHAPTER 7

"Become A Problem Solver"

CHAPTER 7 – TABLE OF CONTENTS

Section		Page
1	Your life Is a Problem-Solving Adventure	264
2	The Art of Negotiating	265
	Exercise: MY Negotiating Skills	269
3	Creativity	270
	Exercise: Time to Create	271
4	Self-Discipline	272
	Exercise: MY Self-Discipline	274
5	Commitment	275
	Exercise: I Believe in ME	278
6	Persistence	279
	Exercise: Persistent Steps	279
7	Problem Solving Made Easy	282
	Exercise: Problem Solving	283
	Exercise: Brainstorming	285
8	Turning Complaints into Objectives	286
	Exercise: MY Complaints	286
	Exercise: Analyzing MY Complaints	287
9	A Theoretical Problem	288
	Exercise: Only One Year to Live	289
10	"Whats"	290
	Exercise: Externals I Try to Change	290

Problem Solver   p. 263

Section 1

Your Life Is a Problem-Solving Adventure

You have, no doubt, heard the advice to refer to *problems* as *challenges*. What does it take to overcome challenges and to win? Not one of us escapes from problems/challenges – so what are the characteristics of an effective problem solver? The most necessary are:

1. Patience
2. Faith
3. Optimism
4. Self-Confidence
5. Creativity
6. Self-Discipline
7. Commitment
8. Persistence
9. Enthusiasm

Enthusiasm

Emerson said about enthusiasm: "Nothing great was ever achieved without enthusiasm." But just what is enthusiasm, and how can you maintain it?

Enthusiasm is defined as ardent zeal or interest, strong excitement of feeling and fervor. It results from a strong belief in yourself and what you do.

Enthusiasm is like a ripple in the water – it spreads! To be enthusiastic, you should *act* enthusiastically, and your emotions will follow.

Ways to be enthusiastic in your thoughts, words and actions:

- Think positive and optimistically
- Smile with your mouth and your eyes
- Emphasize words when you speak
- Associate with other enthusiastic people

Enthusiasm charges your body with energy. An enthusiastic person is hard

Problem Şolver   p. 264

Section 2

The Art of Negotiating

Negotiating is an art that can be learned. Negotiating is not a game. It is a human process in which, when done successfully, everyone wins. Various skills and strategies are required to implement these negotiations on a moment-to-moment basis during the negotiating. The object of negotiating is to secure long-range objectives, not short-term advantages.

As a successful negotiator you need to acquire good skills and techniques. To be a successful negotiator you must start to think in alternatives. Keep in mind negotiation isn't always neat, and it is at times not fair. A knowledge of human behavior is essential to any negotiation. To be successful you should always be prepared. Successful negotiation can depend upon you, your assumptions and your anticipation of the other side's. In a negotiation, each party has needs, direct and indirect, which they want satisfied. Most negotiations do not proceed smoothly.

All parties in a negotiation should come out with some of their needs met. An overwhelmingly one-sided settlement will breed trouble and won't last. A cooperative approach is necessary to attain results that will be long-lasting. Negotiation takes place between human beings. To negotiate successfully you need good people skills.

> *How do you prepare for negotiation?*
>
> *What should you do to be ready for the face-to-face encounter?*
>
> *How can you foresee the strategy of the other side?*

The answer to these questions: **Do your homework.**

Problem Solver   p. 265

Since successful results are what you are looking for, look at and analyze your opponent's strengths and weaknesses. Negotiate problems rather than demands. Our demands are only a one-solution approach to the matter at hand. There may be other solutions. During your negotiation you may want to change your position. If you do not feel you are a strong negotiator, you may want a professional mediator or attorney. A skillful negotiator is alert to the chain of events happening, such as assumptions, positions, new facts, etc. This can be very complicated for a novice.

Another question which is a key factor is the <u>meeting site</u>.

There are three options.

There are advantages and disadvantages to consider when choosing where to meet. Choosing to meet on your turf gives you the psychological advantage of having the other person come to you. There is a comfort level being in your own environment. It saves you time and allows you access to information you may wish to use in the negotiation. You have the power to end the meeting when you wish. Going to your adversary's place lets you focus your full attention on why you are meeting. You won't have to worry about possible interruptions or distractions. You can withhold information – saying you did not bring it along. Another advantage of meeting at his place is he has the responsibility of preparing the meeting site and you may pick up clues about him that would be helpful in negotiating. The last option is to meet at a neutral site. This is the right choice for many negotiations.

The next issue is the negotiating agenda. As the person calling the meeting, your agenda contains the definitions of your terms in your way. Your agenda reveals your position in advance and it permits the other side to prepare for the topics you plan to bring forth.

Problem Solver   p. 266

Attention should be given to each issue to be discussed. The next step is to plan a strategy.

One way is to list the major issues to be discussed first. This is a straight forward style which prevents time from being wasted on minor issues. The second way is to begin with minor issues first so you can start by making some small concessions. Be aware this may be looked at by your opponent as a precedent which he may think it will continue. Since minor issues are easier to resolve, their resolution creates an atmosphere of goodwill. Many people use this approach. The third way to approach the negotiation is to list issues and conditions you feel you both agree on. After stating these you move into issues you must negotiate.

How to open the meeting?

This depends on the people, circumstances, and severity of the negotiation. There are no strict rules. Some people ease into the meeting by discussing a completely irrelevant topic. Another suggestion is to tell a humorous story to help lighten the tension. Another approach some take is making introductory remarks that set forth some of the general principals of negotiation, which are the need for each party to gain something.

Many skills are necessary for you to be a successful negotiator. You need to find accurate information about your opposition. You need a wealth of information in your mind so you may take advantage of any new development in the negotiation. You need patience and must have the ability to keep a clear, cool head about you. You also need to be able to switch gears and be able to remember facts that will be relevant. The skill of listening is also essential. You must really hear what your opposition is saying and not saying. Listening is an art that is worth working at to master. Successful negotiation is a matter of sensitivity and correct timing.

You need to gain insight into how your opposition thinks. The more you know about his method of operating and his psychological approach will be to your benefit. You must be prepared effectively. Successful negotiation involves good communication skills. The usual way to gather information, of course, is to ask questions. Don't be afraid to ask the good questions, the straight-forward questions, the tough questions. Such questions might be:

- *What do you hope to get from this negotiation?*
- *What are your expectations?*
- *What would please you?*
- *What would make you feel good?*

Before the negotiation takes place, ask yourself what you want to accomplish. Be aware of what you are willing to accept for yourself as the outcome. Know what you're willing to give and what you need to keep. Be honest with yourself.

A last suggestion for you to be aware of is the fact that you need to keep focused on your opponent. Stay awake, be aware of the fact that emotions are always involved whenever a negotiation is taking place. Emotions can take over if you're not careful. The factors that affect emotions are intangible. Silent actions, gestures and movements all have something to tell you if you can read body language.

As Emerson stated,

> "What you are speaks so loudly I cannot hear what you say."

EXERCISE

MY Negotiating Skills

Hypothetical essential ingredients for upcoming negotiation:

What do I wish to accomplish?

What is the outcome I'm looking for?

Problem Solver p. 269

Section 3

Creativity

Creativity is a skill you can learn and mastering creativity is not mysterious or magical. It doesn't even require having an artistic aptitude . It does require an open mind.

CREATIVITY IS SIMPLY THE ABILITY TO IMPROVISE AND LOOK FOR AND AT NEW WAYS TO SOLVE CHALLENGES!

You wouldn't be alive today if you didn't have a lot of creativity. You're improvising constantly throughout the day. In fact, finding creative solutions is a vital survival skill.

It's time to come out of your comfort zone and avoid the impulse to reject new ideas before you try them. If you put a little effort into changing your behavior, your routine, or the way you think, it will open new opportunities for you.

Here are some suggestions to help you become more creative:

1. Be willing to risk.
2. Brainstorm.
3. Enjoy the challenge.
4. Be willing to make mistakes.
5. Believe there is a solution to every problem.
6. Look at all your options.
7. Focus and concentrate.
8. Be awake and stay awake.

It takes maverick behavior at times to create what you wish to create, however, being creative is crucial to bring into being your desired results. Make a conscious choice to be the predominant creative force in your life.

Problem Solver   p. 270

EXERCISE

Time to Create

What area of my life could use some creative thinking?

-
-

Problem Solver   p. 271

Section 4

Self-Discipline

What is discipline? It is training that develops self-control, character.

Discipline subjects you to your own rules.

A disciplined person takes control of himself. You become the captain of your own ship. Self-discipline channels your enthusiasm in the right direction.

Discipline is the backbone of any self-improvement.

Discipline should be filled with joy and enthusiasm. Keep your goal in mind when you don't feel like sticking to your plan. Think of the end result of living with your dream realized.

Discipline leads to action.

Discipline is a <u>tool</u> that helps you solve life's problems.

Discipline becomes second nature the more you use it. Discipline is a habit. The more often you use discipline, the more you will have it available to use. It must be practiced constantly; it becomes easier with practice.

As you develop your self-discipline, you can apply it to more difficult tasks in your life.

Self-discipline starts with discipline over your thoughts. You know your thoughts determine your actions. You need to discipline your thoughts before you can discipline your actions. This is an important concept for you to grasp.

Be aware...Your mind is very imaginative in <u>inventing excuses</u>. Discipline your mind.

Problem Solver   p. 272

Your mind and discipline will be in conflict at first. Your mind will try to squash discipline – discipline will try to subdue your mind.

ONCE YOU'RE SUCCESSFUL AT DISCIPLINING YOUR MIND,

YOU HAVE WON.

There are *two* basically different approaches to solving the problems of life:

One is to approach them with feelings.
Another is to approach them with reason and discipline.

| **RIGHT BRAIN** | Feelings | ——————— | Reason – Discipline | **LEFT BRAIN** |

Heart   Head

Some people make decisions based on their feelings.　　Some people make decisions based on reason.

The IDEAL is a "harmonious" blend.

What would you say you tend to make your decisions based on?

- ❏ Your heart
- ❏ Your head

It's a powerful package:

Combine INTELLECT with LOGIC = Your HEART and FEELING

How can you become better at self-discipline?

Do the things you have to do – when they ought to be done... whether you like them or not, whether you feel like doing them or not!

Problem Solver   p. 273

What should you do when you just don't feel like doing what you have to do? – three words my children heard often while growing up:

"JUST DO IT"

The energy you expend complaining about "whatever" could be used to get the job done.

EXERCISE

MY Self-Discipline

Ask yourself these questions:

- *In what areas of my life could I use more discipline?*

___

- *Do I think and make my decisions based on my feelings, or reason?*

___

- *What has this behavior cost me?*

___

- *What will I do in the future?*

___

Problem Solver   p. 274

Section 5

Commitment

Commitment is an *attitude*.

It's a feeling of confidence that, whatever happens, you'll continue to pursue what you want. It's not a self-imposed promise or an obligation. It is a firm belief that what you want is so desirable and so important, it'll be worth doing whatever it takes to get it.

Once you become *committed*, once you become *clear* in your mind that you are willing to do whatever it takes to achieve your goal, life starts creating shortcuts for you. It starts eliminating the need to do certain items you were willing to do. It brings your goal to you without nearly the work or trouble you thought was necessary!

When you set your goal, however, you don't know in advance which items on the list will be eliminated. That's why you *must be willing to do every one*. If you're not sure just what is going to be involved in reaching your goal, just commit 100% to it. You'll find out what it takes soon enough.

Willingness is the key.

With willingness, you will be living your dream; without willingness, your "dreams, goals" will always be out of your reach.

It is your willingness that opens your mind to unlimited possibilities. Without that willingness, it won't work. You can work for years on reaching your goal, however, if you resist doing just *one* item, your dream won't be met. You may as well stop going after that particular goal and choose one for which you are willing to do whatever is asked of you without reservation or hesitation.

When you have the willingness to make a firm commitment, you'll naturally be drawn to doing the things which move you towards the "goal" –

Problem Solver p. 275

your "objective." You have a personal guide which tells you what to do to get what you want. This personal guide works even when you haven't a clue on how to reach your "goal/objective." Listen.

Your responsibility is to FIX THE GOAL clearly in your mind. Make a firm COMMITMENT to reaching it. The direction, the how-to, will become clear. The direction comes out of your intention to achieve your goal.

> You'll know naturally...you'll be drawn to what to do,
>
> when to do it, where, how, who to meet!

What should you commit to? Specific goals, of course; but consider this:

> A commitment to "Mastery" (becoming a Master at something)
>
> will bring you a more fulfilling life.
>
> A "jack of all trades" is seldom good or successful at any.

What would you like to become a Master at?

> A. For a livelihood? _____
>
> B. For your own pleasure? _____

You should consider pursuing what you enjoy. There is a wonderful feeling of pride and satisfaction in becoming an accomplished person in a chosen field.

> *Make a conscious choice of becoming all you were meant to be!*

Once you become a Master, you make whatever you're doing look easy. There is a grace and an appearance of ease, not stress, when you have mastered something.

<u>Mastery:</u>   Medieval French: MAITRE – meaning someone who was exceptionally proficient and skilled, a master of a craft.

Mastery today reflects MAITRE – it means "the capability not only to produce results" but also to "master the principles" underlying the way you produce results. Someone who creates great results only with constant struggle would not be called a master. In mastery, there is a sense of <u>effortlessness, joy and peace</u>. You understand and are commited to go with the natural flow around you.

Personal Mastery involves learning to keep both a personal goal and a clear picture of your current reality. This creates "Creative Tension." Tension by nature seeks resolution. The most natural resolution of this tension is for your current reality to move closer to your personal goal (what you desire).

<u>The "creative orientation": I create my future</u>. You move through life asking, "What do I want to create?" You ask yourself how you caused your circumstances to happen and what you need to do to change them, to take effective action and produce results. You learn from *experiences* and continually improve your *ability*. Knowing what you want in your life – knowing how to make your dream come true and not allowing today's reality to stop you.

Three key concepts to master this discipline:

     1. The ability to articulate your personal goal

     2. The ability to see your current reality clearly

     3. A strong commitment to creating your goals

IT'S YOUR TURN
exercise on next page

Problem Solver   p. 277

EXERCISE

I'm committed to:

I Believe in ME

Problem Solver   p. 278

Section 6

Persistence

Are you a good STARTER but a poor FINISHER? Do you "try" things a lot?

Trying is just a noisy way of <u>not</u> doing something!

Persistence is the opposite of procrastination – it involves sticking to your purpose, especially when it seems inconvenient to do so!

Let this be your new motto:

I WON'T LET ANYTHING STOP ME!

The basis of persistence is the willpower and desire to stick to your commitment. The majority of people are too ready to give up at the first sign of opposition or misfortune. Successful people carry on no matter what. <u>Lack</u> of persistence leads to failure, while persistent goal-oriented actions will ensure success.

Are you persistent enough to follow the advice in this book?

EXERCISE

Persistent Steps

Make a list of the things that will help you be persistent and stay on track to your goals:

1) _____
2) _____
3) _____
4) _____
5) _____

Problem Solver   p. 279

Persistent people reach their goals.
Persistence makes winners!

Persistent people know what they are after, either consciously or subconsciously.

Persistence is an attitude based on an inner conviction.

Knowing with certainty is a main characteristic of persistence.

> *Question:* Do you know with <u>certainty</u> what you want?

How can you learn to have certainty? When you have a goal that is valuable enough by your standards, you can learn certainty by believing in that goal. To succeed, you need faith that you will reach your goal.

Set your mind on the goal and allow nothing to distract you until it's reached. Persistence is a daily decision, an even minute-to-minute decision you must make. You decide whether to persist or give up your goal.

> *Obstacles are the frightful things you see*
> *when you take your mind off your goals!*

Persistence is necessary to snap out of indecision, procrastination, and to overcome obstacles. There are many "obstacles" that may block you from reaching your goals. Some are real blocks, some are imagined blocks:

DO I UNDERSTAND AND ACCEPT THAT SOME THINGS ARE OUT OF MY CONTROL?

> Such as World Events, Weather, Economy

DO I UNDERSTAND AND ACCEPT THAT ONE THING IS TOTALLY UNDER MY CONTROL? MY OWN BELIEFS! *I CONTROL THEM.*

WHAT DO I HAVE CONTROL OVER THAT I'VE BEEN GIVING AWAY?

Problem Solver   p. 280

WHAT SELF-LIMITING BELIEFS DO I HAVE?

WHERE HAVE I HAD BLINDERS ON?

DO I UNDERSTAND THAT "I STOP ME MOST OF THE TIME"?

DO I WANT TO DO ANYTHING ABOUT THIS BEHAVIOR?

WHAT?

_____
_____
_____

Believe in yourself. Believe you will reach your goals.
Believe you deserve it.

Please remember that <u>with persistence</u>,
the most meaningful thing you can live for is to
REACH YOUR FULL POTENTIAL!

Problem Solver   p. 281

Section 7

Problem Solving Made Easy

Problem solving is vital to your success. People who can't solve their own problems don't accomplish much. People who *can* solve their own problems and *"other people's problems"* can write their own ticket to success, and are *sought after*.

> "A problem well stated is a problem half solved."

PROBLEM SOLVING:

No. 1: Write down exactly and completely what the problem is. Include all the actual facts without bias or prejudice. Pretend you are the lawyer from each side presenting all the facts. You as the judge need a <u>description</u> of the problem. You also need an <u>explanation</u>. These are not the same. The description is recording that which is <u>observed</u>. Explanation <u>requires understanding</u>. Description is the *what*; explanation is the *how* and *why*.

No. 2: Write down every possible solution.

No. 3: Decide after deliberation which solution to put into effect. If you have done a thorough job writing down the first two steps, the decision should jump out, it should be clear. If it isn't clear, re-examine each possible solution and alternative. Consider the possibility that possible solutions have been overlooked or omitted. Seek additional innovative and unique decisions.

No. 4: If a decision still does not appear dominant, turn the problem over to your subconscious. Leave it alone for a while. Don't struggle with it. Give it a little time. Sleep on it. If your subconscious does not produce a clear solution, you have a mental block for some psychological reason. You're resisting a solution.

No. 5: Start eliminating the least effective solutions.

Problem Solver   p. 282

No. 6: Talk it out with trusted, knowledgeable people. You may have missed something or don't want to see something. Talking it out will change your focus, and a solution should become clear to you...

No. 7: Decide on the solution.

No. 8: Execute a plan of action.

EXERCISE

Problem Solving

PLAN TO:	DATE I INTEND TO START	DATE IT WILL BE COMPLETED

What Problem Do I Wish to Tackle First?

1. Description and explanation of the problem:

2. Every possible solution/alternative:

a.

b.

c.

d.

e.

Problem Solver   p. 283

3. Do I have a clear decision?   Yes or No: _____
   If the answer is no, what other possible solution:
   _____
   _____

4. Sleep on it.
   _____
   _____

5. Eliminate the least effective solutions. List them:
   _____
   _____
   _____
   _____
   _____
   _____

6. Who can I talk it out with? List:
   _____
   _____
   _____
   _____
   _____
   _____

7. Decide on a solution. The solution is:
   _____
   _____
   _____
   _____
   _____
   _____

Problem Solver   p. 284

EXERCISE

Brainstorming

An additional method of problem solving involves gathering 4 to 6 people together to "brainstorm" on specific problems. Invite people from different work environments, age groups, etc. to ensure varied points of view. Agree to tackle one or two problems for each participant, with all judgments suspended.

Present one problem/challenge at a time, welcome free-form suggestions, positive and negative opinions and arguments to be tossed around like a basketball. Either tape record the session or write down all ideas, even incomplete sentences and key words.

Who would you invite to a brainstorming session?

1)
2)
3)
4)
5)

What problems might benefit from brainstorming?

Problem Solver   p. 285

Section 8

Turning Complaints into Objectives

Complaints could easily become problems unless you transform them into objectives. Your objective has a better chance of becoming a reality if you act positively, take responsibility and set clear goals.

EXERCISE

MY Complaints

This exercise will help you clarify where you are dissatisfied and what solutions you can come up with.

Areas of Life	Complaint	Objective	Action Plan	Time Frame
Career/Job				
Personal Relationship				
Time				
Responsibilities				
Living Arrangements				
Health				
Finances				
Social Life				
Other				

- Be specific. The more specific you are, the more clear it will be to see what needs to be addressed – and what the game plan should be.
- Your complaints are how things are *now*! Describe how you would like things *to be*.
- In the objective column, write what you can do to improve things.
- Express objectives in positive terms. Write what you will do; setting objectives for others is ineffective. *Understand:* Setting objectives for others is ineffective.

Problem Solver   p. 286

EXERCISE

- *HOW DO I FEEL NOW THAT I'VE WRITTEN WHAT I COMPLAIN ABOUT?*

- *WHICH COMPLAINTS ARE TAKING A LOT OF TIME AND ENERGY?*

- *WHICH <u>THREE</u> SHOULD I START WITH?*
1.
2.
3.

- *WHAT WILL BE THE MAIN BENEFITS I'LL ENJOY?*

- *HOW MANY OF MY COMPLAINTS ARE MY TOTAL RESPONSIBILITY? WHICH ONES ARE OUT OF MY CONTROL?*

Section 9

A Theoretical Problem

Imagine you were told you had only one year to live...
What would you do?

The answer to this question excludes long-range planning and forces you to either take care of all the loose ends in your life, or to put all your time into what is most precious to you. Please think about this question and write down on the following page all that you would do.

Consider the following during this exercise:

This is your life. There is no reason to waste your life doing things you don't want to do, especially if you are unhappy. Get out of the rut, open the windows of your mind, look at your life in a new perspective. <u>Be true to yourself, follow your heart</u>. It takes courage. To face the unknown, you must take chances and risks, get out of your comfort zone if you choose to walk the path of your *real self*. Wake up.

As you change, be aware many around you won't like it. You are not supposed to change – they find it threatening. Most people do not like change. Know what usually happens when you try to raise your head above the crowd? Your head gets chopped off. When you try to get out of mediocrity, most people won't rest until you are back down on their level. By having you down on their level, they avoid questioning their own existence.

As you change, you need to get used to the new role you are in. Stop denying yourself your dream. Once you make the commitment to yourself, start telling people about your dream. Make it an obsession until it is so real that the dream starts living and implements itself!

Problem Solver   p. 288

EXERCISE

Only One Year to Live

DATE: _____

I just found out I have only one year to live, so I'm...

_____
_____
_____
_____
_____
_____
_____
_____
_____
_____
_____
_____
_____
_____
_____
_____
_____
_____
_____
_____
_____
_____
_____
_____

Signature: _____

Problem Solver   p. 289

Section 10

"Whats"

Are you spending your life trying to change the *externals*...
Trying to get what you want...
These are the "Whats" in your life.

Please understand "Whats" come and go – "Whats" pass – "Whats" change.

Some examples of "Whats" are:

> money...friends...possessions...opinions...relationships
> dreams...hopes...children...jobs

Your freedom lies in realizing the *how*, the *process*, rather than the content of life. Try not to get caught up in the specifics, the "whats" of your life. Start stepping back and look at the big picture, the process, how it is.

Remember:

It's not what you do – It's how you do it.
It's not what you think – It's how you think.

EXERCISE

What externals are you trying to change?

Externals I Try to Change

Problem Solver   p. 290

Chapter 7 Review Page - Become a Problem Solver

Problem Solver   p. 291

Problem Solver   p. 292

CHAPTER 8

"The Power of Your Subconscious Mind"

CHAPTER 8 – TABLE OF CONTENTS

Section		Page
1	Your Conscious Mind	297
2	Your Subconscious Mind	299
3	Your Subconscious Is Your Control System	301
4	Subconscious Needs	303
	Exercise: Subconscious Needs of People I Wish to Help	305
	Exercise: MY Subconscious Needs	306
5	Mental Picture Power	307
6	Turn Off Unwanted Mental Pictures	310
	Exercise: Negative Mental Pictures	311
7	Thoughts Are "Things"	312
	Exercise: My Thoughts Create Reality	316
8	Creative Visualization	317
	Exercise: Creative Visualization	321
	Exercise: MY No. 1 Priority	323
	Exercise: Visualization	324
9	Imagine Your Future into Reality	325
	Exercise: Controlled Mental Pictures	328
10	"As If "	329
	Exercise: As If	333

Subconscious Mind   p. 295

Section 1

Your Conscious Mind

Your conscious mind is in charge as you read these words. The rational ability to think and reason, coupled with self-awareness, differentiates man from animals. The opposite of being conscious, awake and alert is being *un*conscious. So how does the conscious mind differ from the *sub*conscious mind, and why is it important?

The consciousness of each waking moment affects the mental activities just below the threshold of awareness. Ideas, beliefs, mental pictures are created on a conscious level and then "stored" subconsciously, where they can subsequently affect your thoughts and behavior, at a later time, WITHOUT ENTERING CONSCIOUS AWARENESS!

All parts of foolishness as well as wisdom are in your subconscious mind. It is important for you to realize that you *create* what's there, and you can *control* its effect.

Your conscious mind can deliberately project your mental pictures upon the "picture screen" of your subconscious. You can consciously visualize your mental pictures and you can consciously control your mental pictures.

It is essential for you to take control of what you're feeding your mind. If you are not vigilant, your mind will wander and unhealthy, unproductive, negative thoughts creep in. You can stop this mind poison – it's not healthy and will allow worry and unwanted thoughts to be fed to your subconscious.

What unhealthy, unproductive, negative thoughts do I entertain?

- _____
- _____
- _____
- _____

Subconscious Mind   p. 297

When the spark of mind first flickered into being, primeval man began to think things out and plan what to do instead of acting by impulse or necessity. The activity, ingenuity and creativeness of the human mind led from one discovery and achievement to another, until today the intellect of man probes beyond our immediate environment to the encompassing universe. Our ability to bring ideas into manifestation has transformed every aspect of our lives.

All that we are is the result of what we have thought;
it is made by our thoughts.

Your conscious thoughts help to create your reality:

Your Conscious Mind provides the <u>management</u> which decides what you want to acquire and what you want to become. These are decisions that you deliberately make. Your conscious mind (the management part of your mind) transmits its instructions through mental pictures to your Subconscious Mind, which is your "<u>Life Manufacturing Factory</u>."

Your subconscious mind accepts without question your mental pictures, whatever they are, as <u>absolute instructions</u> to produce them as your life, and proceeds to do so in the same miraculous manner that it operates your heartbeat, your breathing, and all of your life functions. Your subconscious mind has the unlimited means and power to guide you to or attract to you whatever you intensely and consistently project as mental pictures of your life-goal. In fact, it cannot do otherwise. This is the Law of Consistency, which requires that your mind commands (mental pictures) which you "plant as seeds" in your subconscious produce exactly what you plan – so that what you harvest is consistent with what you plant.

Section 2

Your Subconscious Mind

This is the part of your mind which operates regardless of our conscious control. It can be directed by your conscious mind, using mental pictures visualized by conscious thought. Your subconscious mind performs many functions. It's in complete control of your life. It's in complete control of your bodily functions (everything which your living requires). It is the "something" which connects to infinity – it's the channel to Infinite Intelligence and Infinite Power (to the extent man can understand it).

Your subconscious is your channel to all of the means and power you ever will need for anything. Your subconscious is a memory storehouse which retains every thought and image you ever had mentally pictured – even if your conscious mind has completely forgotten. This is proven by the capability of psychoanalysis to probe your forgotten past all the way back through your early years. Your mental pictures – past and present – are arranged through your subconscious to become the "building blocks of your life," each in its own size and importance according to the intensity of each mental picture when it was projected into your subconscious.

Everyone has a "self-image" and we become what we envision (mentally picture) ourselves to be. What you are now is the result of the kind and intensity of mental pictures which you deliberately or carelessly projected into your subconscious throughout your life – for better or worse.

Your subconscious mind is powerful.
Your subconscious mind does not judge nor does it ask questions.
It obeys and moves you to what you believe, what you tell it.
It does not know the difference between what is real or unreal.

Your subconscious will guide you to or attract to you whatever you want – in direct proportion to the intensity and frequency of your mental pictures of your actually possessing whatever you want.

Subconscious Mind   p. 299

So...If it's $10 million you want, you must intensely, frequently project into your life-guidance subconscious vivid, impressive mental pictures of you actually possessing it.

For your self-image (mental picture) to be "real" in your imagination, it must be so intense that it dominates your constant thought and, therefore, dominates your life-guidance instructions to your subconscious.

Subconscious Mind   p. 300

Section 3

Your Subconscious Is Your Control System

Start to learn to use the methods of directing your subconscious.

The fact is that your thoughts (mental pictures) create corresponding physical changes.

Your life is the product of your thoughts. *When something happens in the mind, it also happens in your body.* This is called "psycho-physical parallelism" – that is, mind and body are always parallel, for they are two aspects of one and the same substance...The New You.

Every minute, a part of you is gone – forever – 3 billion worn-out cells. Obviously, you cannot do this consciously. The building of a New You at the rate of 3 billion new cells a minute is a function of your subconscious.

This is why you can change yourself through your subconscious.

Not only does your subconscious control the creating of the New You, but it receives 600,000 items, impulse-connected bits of knowledge, every minute from your nervous system through your brain.

Your conscious mind cannot handle or even be aware of 600,000 items of knowledge a minute. The use and/or memory storage of this vast inflow of sensory knowledge is also the function of your subconscious mind.

This is why I keep stressing the importance of the subconscious and why it is capable of creating a "New You" from these vital new "materials," the use and control of which is the function of your subconscious.

I can't emphasize enough the need for and the methods of directing your-subconscious to reach your goals.

Subconscious Mind   p. 301

Your subconscious – Your <u>Life-Building</u> – and Your <u>Life-Control System</u>...
LEARN TO USE IT.

The following methods will help.

To literally "computerize" your subconscious, making its principal objective to guide you to or attract the opportunities you need to reach your goals, use these methods:

<u>Vivid Mental Pictures</u>   <u>Goal Commands</u>   <u>Self-Hypnosis</u>
<u>Silent Chants</u>   <u>Meditation</u>

These methods focus your mind on your goals. You must intensify your mental pictures so that they will be your constant, dominant thought. You want all of your principal thinking related directly or indirectly to your goals.

1. **Vivid Mental Pictures**
   Mental pictures are specific instructions to your subconscious mind.
   Examples: _____

2. **Goal Commands**
   Keep your goal commands short and forceful.
   Examples: _____

3. **Self-Hypnosis**

4. **Silent Chants (Affirmations)**
   Examples: _____

5. **Meditation**

Subconscious Mind   p. 302

Section 4

Subconscious Needs

Subconscious Bonding (a deeply felt connection)
occurs when you fulfill the subconscious needs of others.

There are two kinds of Vision:

A. Physical – Objects you see with your eyes which can be touched
B. Mental, Mental Subconscious Power – Your insight, which enables you to see with your subconscious perception (an entirely new dimension of life)

It reveals unlimited opportunities which have remained hidden from your physical vision.

SUBCONSCIOUS NEEDS OF EVERYONE:

Deep, insistent, subconscious needs motivate all people, causing them to do whatever they do in their attempts to fulfill their subconscious needs.

Your Mental Vision (insight) enables you to see the <u>inner</u> person and the deep subconscious needs that crave to be fulfilled.

By fulfilling a subconscious need of someone, you activate a subconscious "positive response" which bonds his positive subconscious power with yours.

Each time this happens, it multiplies your personal Positive Power greatly.

Everyone has many and very complex subconscious needs. Everybody's subconscious needs are constantly and desperately striving to be met.

Subconscious Mind   p. 303

Fill these needs, and you will be on their most-wanted list!

EVERYONE Needs to

- Feel Approval
- Feel Accepted
- Feel Agreed with (supports the ego)
- Feel Admired
- Feel Appreciated
- Feel Important
- Be Right
- Have Attention
- Be Needed
- Get Outside Help Sometime During Their Life
- Be Respectful
- Be Valued

Once you fill these needs, ***bonding takes place.***

EXERCISE

Subconscious Needs of People I Wish to Help

Name	Need Identified	What Can I Do to Meet This Need?

Subconscious Mind   p. 305

EXERCISE

MY Subconscious Needs

MY SUBCONSCIOUS NEEDS THAT ARE BEING MET:
_____
_____
_____
_____
_____
_____
_____

MY SUBCONSCIOUS NEEDS THAT ARE NOT BEING MET:
_____
_____
_____
_____
_____
_____
_____

WHAT CAN I DO TO GET THESE NEEDS MET?
_____
_____
_____
_____
_____
_____
_____
_____
_____

Subconscious Mind   p. 306

Section 5

Mental Picture Power

*"You will become what you mentally picture.
Your future will be what you mentally picture it to be."*

YOUR THOUGHTS – YOUR MENTAL PICTURES
DETERMINE YOUR FUTURE.

You think with mental pictures – every thought you have is a mental picture projected into your subconscious.

Every mental picture is your instruction to your subconscious to guide your life in the direction of your goal until it becomes reality.

Buddha taught: "All that we are is the result of what we have thought."

Your thoughts are mental pictures projected into the subconscious which guides you to – or attracts to you – your self-image. Everybody has a self-image and becomes what they envision themselves to be.

William James of Harvard wrote,
"Belief" (an intense mental picture/creates the actual fact)
Emerson wrote, "Thoughts" (mental pictures rule the world)

Did you realize how powerful your thoughts are?

To understand the nature of the mind is to acquire awesome power.

Your mental pictures are brought into reality by being converted into power by your subconscious.

You govern your life through your mental pictures.

Whatever you pay attention to will grow more important in your life. There is no limit to the kinds of changes that AWARENESS can produce.

Think for a moment of planting a garden in the spring. You can only harvest in the fall that which you planted in the spring. The same rules apply to your mind.

"You can only harvest what you plant."

Just like a garden, you can't plant daisies and expect roses to grow!

Start planting (in your subconscious) what you want to have in your life.

Mental pictures of good health, wealth, whatever it is you wish. Your goal-producing subconscious is always listening.

I WISH TO HAVE:
_____
_____
_____
_____
_____
_____
_____
_____
_____

Mental pictures of wealth can only produce wealth. The Law of Consistency will not permit mental pictures of wealth to produce poverty!

Start thinking of your "Thoughts as Mental Pictures."

The "Picture Screen of your Mind is your Subconscious."

Your subconscious "remembers," and with its goal-seeking powers guides you or attracts you to whatever you repeatedly and intensely project on its "picture screen."

Subconscious Mind   p. 308

The mental "picture screen" of your subconscious is your life-guidance system which can and will materialize your mental pictures into reality.

Learn how to control your mental pictures to reach your life goals and live the life you wish.

Consistently picture what you want so your subconscious mind can work on it.

Without a clear mental picture, you cannot get it, you need a blueprint, a road map.

The subconscious mind does not respond to fuzzy pictures.

You will start guiding your life with mental pictures.

A mental movie is formed from continuous sequences of mental pictures.

You are the *star* – the *producer* – the *director*. You control the mental movie which you project on "the screen" of your subconscious.

You choose the kind of ★ <u>star</u> ★ you will be in your own mental movie, which will become "<u>Your Life</u>." *You* determine your future.

THE LAW OF CONSISTENCY

The "Law of Consistency" will cause you to be in <u>real life</u> exactly the kind of person you picture yourself to be <u>in your mind</u>. This law of nature requires that you can only become what is consistent with how you "see" yourself.

Keep your dominant thoughts positive, success oriented. If your dominant thoughts are of success, you will constantly replay in your mental movie mind a mental movie of success. You as the "<u>star</u>" will "act out" in your mental movie a great performance as a success.

Then you can "only" be a success in real Life because

Your Real Life must be consistent with what you mentally picture it to be.

Section 6

Turn Off Unwanted Mental Pictures

You can deliberately control your mental pictures if you persist.

When you do not deliberately control the mental movies which are the picture sequence of your thought-flow, the uncontrolled thoughts, uncontrolled mental pictures, fill all mental spaces not filled by controlled thoughts. Your uncontrolled daydreams are present, and usually, they are mental picture situations of worry, fear, etc., which have been suppressed in your subconscious and which your subconscious takes the first opportunity to release (feed back) into your conscious thought. This repeats and reinforces **NEGATIVE** thoughts to become your life-guidance – with negative consequences.

Since whatever is suppressed in your subconscious is "undesirable" (or it would not be suppressed), the worst thing you can do to your future is to "repeat" and "reinforce" uncontrolled mental pictures of worry, fear, anxieties, etc. into the subconscious management of your life and the materialization of your future.

It's vital that you "turn off" negative and undesirable mental pictures.

The greatest misfortune that can come to a human being is to lose "inner peace." No outer force can rob you of it. It is your own undesirable thoughts and actions that rob you of it.

Whenever a dreadful experience occurs, deal with it by asking, "How did my mental pictures contribute to this reality?" If you have the power to create or allow unhappiness, you also have the power to *un*create it.

Subconscious Mind   p. 310

This exercise will show you how to:

Relax...Close Your Eyes...
Imagine Heavy Fog – I find it relaxing

Let your mind be filled with total fog. Blank out all mental pictures. Maintain total mental fog until your mind is relaxed and quiet, in which no mental picture can be seen. You have achieved the advanced mental-emotional level of a quiet mind.

Blank out by blocking out all mental pictures

The objective is to achieve non-stimulation.

I like to imagine heavy fog. You envelop all mental pictures in a heavy fog which completely fills your mind, "fogging out" mental pictures by filling your mind with wisps of fog, which mentally turn into deeper clouds of fluffy fog, and then into heavy fog which totally obscures all mental pictures. Your mind is filled with dense fog through which you mentally can see nothing – *no mental pictures.*

Once your mind is clear, state what disturbing, negative, or mental pictures you wish to have stop.

WHAT DISTURBING, NEGATIVE, MENTAL PICTURES DO I WISH TO HAVE STOP?
_____
_____
_____

WHAT WILL I REPLACE THE NEGATIVE MENTAL PICTURES WITH?
_____
_____
_____

Promise to me: I WILL BECOME GOOD AT THIS AND USE IT EACH DAY!

Subconscious Mind

Section 7

Thoughts Are "Things"

Many people regard the non-physical as non-real, assuming that if they can't see, touch, taste, feel, or measure something, then it doesn't exist. If you are one of these people, please consider this:

Your <u>thoughts</u> fall into the <u>non-physical category</u>. You can't see, touch, taste, feel or perceive them objectively. Yet you "know" your thoughts exist because <u>you think them</u>. For the most part, people deny the objective reality of their thoughts as things.

Enlightened thinkers have recognized that thoughts are indeed "real."

They believe thoughts possess an objective reality. Everything that becomes a reality starts with a thought. Thoughts are powerful. You have heard the saying, "What you think about comes about." Thoughts are real – as real as anything else in this world.

We are the masters of our fate because we have the power to control our thoughts! When you persistently think something, it will eventually transform into reality.

"Reality" perceived – or created – by your mind consists of the same chemical and electrical processes as thoughts, fantasies and dreams. A scientist examining your brain would be unable to distinguish whether you were actually seeing a piece of chocolate cake or just imagining it. Which is reality to the subconscious? Both are!

Everything you need in life already exists in your head!
All reality in life is what you perceive it to be!
Thought is cause.
Experience is effect.
If you don't like the effects in your life,
you have to change the nature of your thinking.
Your reality is not as rigid as you might believe.

Subconscious Mind   p. 312

Things attract other things through the magnetic power of "attraction."

*The more similar the things are,
the stronger their attraction to one another.*

Whenever you think something, the thought immediately attracts its physical equivalent. I'll give you a few examples: Think about food, and before long you're eating. Think about purchasing a car; soon you find yourself looking at car ads, stopping by showrooms, test driving cars, and eventually owning and driving that car.

When you think of something, let's say it's a personal fortune of two million dollars, that thought immediately begins attracting its physical equivalent. It immediately begins drawing two million dollars towards itself, towards you, the holder of that thought. Now, in physical reality, two million dollars may seem a long, long way from where you are. The prospect of your physically having two million dollars may seem dim. Right?

Wrong.

When you think of having two million dollars and commit yourself to having it, the money begins making its own way toward you. Once it begins, it moves faster and faster. I have multi-millionaire friends who have had this happen. The first million took them some years to make; however, once that happened, the rest started coming in at an increasingly fast rate.

Once the <u>momentum</u> has begun, it is difficult to stop. When things begin moving toward each other, they move at an increasing rate.

The process is under way once you begin it in your mind, in your thoughts.

The things you want start flowing towards you quickly and more easily as time goes by.

This is really known as "a sweet spot in time." It's amazing – the right opportunities are presented to you. The right people appear that propel you towards your goal. A power is felt by you that attracts what and who should be part of this wonderful process. You have all heard the sayings, "money begets money" and "success breeds success." It's true. People start to sense this in you and want to be around you. People like to deal with winners and be part of a winning team.

What you think about comes about.
So, upgrade your thinking!

In objective reality, the thought of winning <u>attracts the physical counterpart of winning</u> – the victory itself. The <u>thought of success attracts its physical counterpart</u>, be it the close of a sale, losing weight, a new career, or whatever "success" means to you.

The world you live in is subjective. It is responsive to you and obeys your <u>thoughts</u>, feelings and attitudes.

Attitude is more important than facts!!

We have a choice every day regarding what attitude we will embrace for that day: we create it with our thoughts.

The world is empty until you step on the stage and make it happen. By your thoughts, words, actions, you give the world meaning and fill it with life! The world takes on the meaning you give it – and, therefore, you are responsible for the meaning of your life.

Since you now know that your thoughts are <u>as real as this book</u>, you have to educate them so that you create the reality you want. Your thoughts are much more valuable than the "reality" you perceive outside of yourself because they can **"CREATE" REALITY**. This workbook cannot change reality, but your <u>thoughts</u> can. Your <u>thoughts</u> and <u>words</u> are the powerful tools you use to transform reality and to create your world.

*The more expansive your thoughts,
the more expansive the reality you create!*

What we perceive, the way we see things, is mostly for our own convenience.

Things at a distance are not really smaller, and solid things are not really solid. Everything is ENERGY, including you and me and everything we think. Thinking consumes, creates and converts energy.

Thoughts can influence things because thoughts are energy, and energy can influence things.

Thoughts Are Things

Things I Think About Come About

Subconscious Mind   p. 315

EXERCISE

Write down things you wish to bring into your life:

MY Thoughts Create Reality

Subconscious Mind   p. 316

Section 8

Creative Visualization
(the power of creative vision)

Scholars have found that much of our potential for creating reality resides in our ability to think in images. Images precede words. Creative vision can be defined as a combination of imagination and intuition, and it has been responsible for all of civilization's greatest advances.

You can harness the power of creative vision by seeing in your mind exactly what you expect to see in reality – by holding a sharp and focused mental picture of the goal you want to achieve.

CREATIVE VISUALIZATION WORKS BEACAUSE
REALITY AND ILLUSION ARE THE SAME.

You visualize the image of the reality you want to create in your mind. Through this, you create an image and likeness to reality. This process works because "reality" on Earth has a tendency to fashion itself according to the mold created by your visualization.

MENTAL PICTURES SOONER OR LATER CREATE REALITY BECAUSE ILLUSION
AND REALITY CONSIST OF THE SAME BUILDING BLOCKS AND, THEREFORE,
INFLUENCE AND DETERMINE EACH OTHER.

The illusion in your mind (above)
determines
the illusion (below) "reality" in your life.

First, you must see and believe it in your mind;
then, you'll get it in reality.

Subconscious Mind   p. 317

Creative Vision has Unlimited Power

It's a tool available to you – you decide to use it to build or destroy!

It's the tool that shaped your life right now.

It's the tool that can make your DREAMS COME TRUE!

Creative Visualization generates pathways through your mind and makes you familiar with your future.

The process is simple:

Athletes practice visualization constantly. Runners visualize themselves crossing the finish line. They see the clock stating the minutes they wish to finish the race in. They memorize the course in their mind. They have mentally run and completed the race thousands of times using creative visualization.

It works with <u>material</u> things as well as <u>thoughts</u>, <u>ideas</u>, <u>concepts</u>.

Using visualization, you create a potential world within you.

Vision is the ability to see your <u>goals</u>, your <u>future</u>, as they ideally should be – the ideal picture and idea of yourself – your family – your work – your home. It's knowing with absolute certainty where you are going and what you're all about.

Before you start on your successful journey, you need to have the <u>vision of what your life is about</u>, what you want your life, your world, to look like.

MOST PEOPLE SPEND MORE TIME PLANNING their vacation than they do planning their life. Before they start out, they have a destination in mind and an itinerary. You cannot expect to reach your destination without plans. You also want the best plan to make your trip as pleasurable as possible – you may run into roadblocks, so it's always wise to have an alternate plan. They send for information videos, catalogues and maps to get them to their destination. Some people have a vision in their mind of where they wish to go. Some people don't know where they want to go on vacation, so they explore new avenues, searching for an interesting trip.

Ask yourself: Why would you not put energy, thought and a plan in place for the "<u>Journey of your Life</u>"?

Isn't it time to stop and think of where you are – where you wish to go?

STOP LETTING LIFE JUST HAPPEN TO YOU!

"Vision" is the first creative step towards reality.

As you give your affirmations, <u>you need to create a vision</u>. Look at <u>affirmations</u> as the creative tool to build your world.

Your vision is the exact blueprint you, as the builder, need.

<u>Start to Visualize</u> *the things you wish to create.*
Always put your <u>vision</u> into the <u>present time</u>.
<u>Envision</u> *everything to be true for you right this moment.*

Thank the Universe for bringing it to you as if you had it already.

Visualization Life Affirmation is a form of programming:

- It works because of the Law of Attraction.
- <u>The Law of Attraction</u> says that <u>perfect vision creates perfect reality</u>.

YOU CONTROL YOUR MENTAL VISION.

- You can use it for whatever purpose you like!
- When creating your vision, be precise!
- Only ask for things that are for the good of the greatest number of people. Always leave an opening for something **better**.

State: "<u>This</u>, or <u>something better</u>"

Subconscious Mind   p. 319

THE IDEAL SCENE EXERCISE

Envision your future the way you would like to see it!

Look at every single facet – paint an exact and extremely detailed picture of this "wishful thinking," the reality you desire. Leave nothing out. Notice details of this vision – the picture on the wall, the music playing, the smells, etc. Every single detail.

Remember: The Law of Attraction states:

> "<u>Like attracts like</u>." The more precise your mental picture is, the sooner you will attract that reality and the nearer to your original "vision" it will be.

Start by directing your "vision" to the area of your life that you would like to change the most. Relationship, home, work…

In the chosen area, create the "ideal scene" as you would like to see it.

WHAT YOU REALLY WANT FROM LIFE
• CREATIVE VISUALIZATION EXERCISE •

What would you really like to have?

<u>Imagine</u>: You were sent a thousand-page catalog and you can order anything life has to offer. The items in your catalog don't cost money, but they have a price. Some say that it is very little for what you receive, some say it's a lot. The price you pay is your life – you can get what you want, but "<u>you have to pay the price</u>."

Close your eyes – Write down about 20 <u>things you want</u>: material things, immaterial things.

Example: I want: a partner, good health, good friends, a good job, love, money, world peace, etc.

It's important to know exactly what you want from life before you proceed in setting goals. Now highlight your top 20 priorities.

Subconscious Mind   p. 320

EXERCISE

Creative Visualization

s20 Things I want in my life:

1.
2.
3.
4.
5.
6.
7.
8.
9.
10.
11.
12.
13.
14.
15.
16.
17.
18.
19.
20.

Subconscious Mind   p. 321

CREATE THE IDEAL SCENE
for your 20 priorities

1. Visualize you already have your #1 priority item.
2. Visualize the process of acquiring it and the situation and scenery in actually possessing it.
   (Write and draw pictures of how it looks on the form provided)
   Use the present tense when doing this activity.

   Ex: <u>Write</u>: I own a cottage on the beach. Put in all the details. Get the feeling of enjoying it and using it. Draw or cut out photos of
what you want.

By doing this exercise, you are feeding your subconscious mind the information of what needs to be produced. Your subconscious mind is powerful. It does not judge if you should have what you tell it – its job is to see that you get it, to carry out your orders. Visualization of every detail is very important.

EXAMPLE: **WORK**

<u>CHOOSE</u> the ideal scene – Describe your occupation. Start with simple things: Where do you work? How long does it take you to get there? Where is your office? Describe the furniture. Who are you working with? Exactly how much money do you make a week? Envision your paycheck.

After you have shaped your ideal physical environment, direct your attention to your feelings: How do you feel? What are your emotions? Do you smile? Do you feel great? Describe how your body feels. Do you have a lot of energy? Etc., etc.

CREATIVE VISUALIZATION WORKS

Nothing that the mind can conceive is impossible.

You need to plan, execute your plan, to bring it into the physical world.

Subconscious Mind   p. 322

EXERCISE

My No. 1 priority is:

MY No. 1 Priority

Assignment: *Go back and look at page 19. Did your No. 1 priority change?*

Subconscious Mind   p. 323

Miracles are for believers, and believing means staying with your dream through any challenges, no matter what they are.

Since your reality is <u>your</u> dream, you can dream it any way you want. You can change the script at any time. You can change your circumstances more easily than you might think. THERE ARE NO LIMITS.

Take time to daydream, fantasize, relax and think about what you want to create. Practice thinking in new, unlimited ways. Enlarge your vision of what is possible.

EXERCISE

Visualization

These pictures and reminders help me see what I want my life to look like in many areas. You may work on more than one at a time.

Subconscious Mind   p. 324

Section 9

Imagine Your Future into Reality

YOUR MENTAL PICTURES ARE OF GREAT CONSEQUENCE TO YOU BECAUSE THEY WILL BECOME YOUR LIFE.

Your mind is like a camera. Your mind makes mental pictures of whatever is exposed to it – and those mental pictures will subsequently become your life!

So...

Expose your mind to whatever you want in your life. (Your mind camera will make a mental picture of whatever is exposed to it.) Use objects that represent what you want.

Suggestion: Make a scrapbook; cut out pictures from magazines; visit places; do related activities – read on the subject; make a bulletin board of things you want; borrow items; send for brochures; subscribe to magazines related to what you want; get to know people who are living the life you wish to live.

Whatever your goal, hold in your mind mental pictures of the kind of objects, locations, activities, people associated with what you want.

And remember...

The only way you can make a picture – with a camera or in your mind – is by <u>EXPOSURE</u>. (Mental pictures require constant exposure.)

*Your exposure must be consistent with your life goals.
You must expose yourself to the objects, people, circumstances, ideas, thoughts, plans, situations that will bring you to your desired goals.*

Subconscious Mind   p. 325

It is vital that your exposure be consistent with your life goals. You cannot expose your mental camera to activities and thoughts associated with failure and expect it to produce mental pictures of success to guide your subconscious. You must be deliberately selective in choosing the associates, activities, reading, everything to which you expose your mind because each and every exposure will be a mental picture. And each mental picture will guide your life to be consistent with the exposure. If you are aimless and indifferent in thinking about your life goals, your subconscious will be equally aimless and indifferent in directing you to your goal or attracting-what you want.

I understand...

- My mind is continually running mental movies;
- My mental movies consist of mental pictures on the "picture screen" of my subconscious;
- My mental pictures impress themselves on my subconscious mind permanently;
- My subconscious uses my mental pictures "cybernetically," which means my mental pictures become my life-guidance system;
- Therefore, my mental pictures determine my future because they guide me to and attract to me more opportunities, the right people, whatever I need to reach my goals.

You have heard the rich get richer and the poor get poorer – *think about this!* The rich mentally picture what they physically see – the wealth that surrounds them. Their mental pictures are of wealth; they think "rich," so they get richer. They are surrounded by wealth.

The poor mentally picture what they see – poverty. Their mental pictures are of poverty, so they think "poor," and they get poorer.

*So...*The poor **must change their mental pictures** and impress mental pictures of money, success (whatever they want) into their subconscious mind.

What you physically see in your surroundings become mental pictures. However, these visually produced mental pictures DO NOT HAVE TO BE DOMINANT and can be subjugated by the much more powerful mental pictures you _deliberately_ produce in your imagination.

You _can_ and you _must_ deliberately produce much more powerful dominant, vivid, controlled mental pictures in your imagination in order to have materialize in your life that which you want.

You _can_ and you _must_ (I repeat) visualize mental pictures by deliberately imagining them.

Because you can produce mental pictures deliberately – simply by imagining them – you can control your mental pictures, impressing them permanently into your subconscious.

Imagine the mental pictures of what you desire:

repeatedly – constantly – intensely

Your subconscious uses your mental pictures (good or bad) to cybernetically direct your life (for better or worse) so that whatever you picture becomes real.

The mental pictures in your subconscious provide motivational guidance through preconditioning your attitude. This prompts you to act in a predetermined manner to achieve the objective which you repeatedly – constantly – intensely – mentally picture.

> _Your mental pictures guide you. You must respond to their guidance._
> _You cannot be guided if you do not respond._
> _You must respond by **DOING** (not by waiting for a miracle)._

By simply reading this book, you will not succeed. You must do what it teaches you to do.

Once you keep your mind filled with controlled mental pictures of what you want, your subconscious cannot be filled with uncontrolled, harmful, negative, disturbing thoughts. Most people do not understand this, and they leave their minds open for negative thoughts – mental pictures of what they <u>do not</u> want.

EXERCISE

THE CONTROLLED MENTAL PICTURES I WILL START IN MY MIND:

Controlled Mental Pictures

1. _____
2. _____
3. _____
4. _____
5. _____
6. _____
7. _____
8. _____
9. _____
10. _____

I now understand my mental pictures guide me.

I will respond to their guidance.

I will start *doing* what is necessary to bring about the future I wish.

Subconscious Mind   p. 328

Section 10

"As If"

IMAGINE "AS IF"...you are living the life you wish right now.

Since you now understand your thoughts are a continuous series of mental pictures – your thoughts are a mental movie – You are the "star" of your mental movie – the part you cast yourself in you will discover that you are actually living in Real Life. The reason for this is because the part you play in your mental movie – *failure or success* – is the way you give directions to your subconscious.

Your mental movie is your conscious mind's way of instructing your always receptive subconscious:

> *"This is what I want to become...This is what I want to have... This is what I want to do in real life."*

Remember, your subconscious is "cybernetic," which means "goal achieving." Think of it as a "guided missile" – just like a guided missile, it will seek and reach whatever goals are programmed into its guidance system.

Your subconscious mind's function and goal is to materialize into the reality of your life whatever you intensely and constantly picture in your mental movie, which is the guidance director of your subconscious.

Your subconscious can "attract" you to or guide you to whatever is necessary – opportunities, people, etc. – to enable you to attain your life goals.

The power of your subconscious to influence or actually <u>ARRANGE</u> the circumstances and events which materialize your intense, constant mental pictures into reality is difficult for most people to understand.

> *This has been the teaching of <u>all</u> religions throughout the centuries. It is proven over and over by psychology, psychiatry and behavioral scientists.*

Subconscious Mind   p. 329

As a man thinketh, "so he will become" because man is destined to become the reality of his mental pictures.

William L. James did much work on the psychology of "AS IF" and illuminated its unlimited possibilities in personal goal achievement.

Used effectively, it will enable you to become the kind of person you want to be – and attain your life goals – and get whatever you want in life.

The 3 AS IFs: IMAGINE – THINK – ACT

Imagine "As If"...
By doing this, you actually imagine your future into reality!

Psychologists suggest that you constantly visualize a mental picture of your ideal self-image. This mental picture of your "Ideal You" must be a mental movie of you looking, acting, talking and doing everything "As If" you already have become the kind of person you wish to become. In your imagination, you must clearly and intensely "see" yourself "exactly" and in as much detail as possible – "as if" you already have become your ideal you. In your imagination, you must "vividly live" your future as you wish it to be. Start now doing this intensely, continuously in every moment of your day.

YOU WILL ACTUALLY BECOME THE KIND OF PERSON YOU WISH TO BE.

In philosophical terms, "Our Life is what our thoughts make it."

– *The words of Marcus Aurelius of Ancient Rome*

Or in the terms of William James, "Belief (constant thought expressed through mental pictures) creates the Actual Fact."

Or in terms of modern logic and the "Law of Consistency," "Action (in this case, becoming) must be consistent with constant THOUGHT."

When you think "as if," you activate the mental pictures into reality through the power of positive thinking. Dr. Norman Vincent Peale, a leader in the field of the power of positive thinking (who taught "think success") said, "Think and visualize success and you set in motion the powerful force of the realized wish. When the mental picture attitude is strongly enough held, it actually seems to control conditions and circumstances. A mental picture strongly held does control conditions and circumstances. You will set in motion the power force of the realized wish."

> *When you think as if you are successful, you will acquire the all-important, all-powerful "<u>success attitude</u>."*

"Success or failure in business is caused more by mental attitude than by mental capabilities."

– stated by Dr. Walter Scott, psychologist
and president of Northwestern University.

I believe this is also true in your personal life.

Wish to be successful and rich?

> *Start to THINK as if you <u>are</u> successful and rich –*
>
> *think SUCCESS, think RICH.*

Constantly picture yourself being rich. Constantly visualize in your imagination the wealth you want, the fine possessions, the trips you'll take, the homes you'll own, the activities you'll enjoy, and how you will help others (how your being rich will benefit others is very important). Become <u>money conscious</u>. Impress into your subconscious over and over the forceful goal command – $10 million – or whatever you decide upon.

Action seems to follow feeling, but really action and feelings go together... by regulating the ACTION which is under the more direct control of the will, we can indirectly regulate the FEELING which is not.

By ACTING as if we feel happy, or confident, or strong, we actually cause ourselves to feel the way we "act." If your confidence is lost, "Act" as if you feel confident, and you can indirectly regulate the feeling. People used to believe "only" that Action followed feeling. So, if you didn't feel confident, you acted that way. Of course, this remains true. William James announced a new psychological concept...

Not only does ACTION follow feeling
but
Feeling follows Action.

So, if you feel unhappy, you can act "as if" you are cheerful, and thus change your feelings of unhappiness to feelings of cheerfulness – to be consistent with acting "as if" you are cheerful. Again, the "Law of Consistency" at work.

When you act "as if" (however you want to feel), then to be <u>consistent</u>, you will feel the way you act. This enables you to change and control your feelings, your emotions, your mind moods – simply by Acting "As If" you can *turn off* undesirable and self-damaging feelings.

So to review for you, the three parts to remember are:

- **Imagine "as if"**
- **Think "as if"**
- **Act "as if"**

Then, whatever you imagine "as if" will become a reality because your imagination thoughts and actions are goal commands to your subconscious, which will direct you to or attract to you whatever is consistent with your dominant thoughts and actions.

EXERCISE

I WILL START TO IMAGINE — THINK — ACT AS IF!
I will write how I will look, speak, act, dress, in clear terms and in the present tense:

As If

Chapter 8 Review Page - The Power of Your Subconscious Mind

Subconscious Mind   p. 335

Subconscious Mind p. 336

CHAPTER 9

"Carpe Vitam!"
(Seize Life)

CHAPTER 9 – TABLE OF CONTENTS

Section		Page
1	Personal Magic	341
2	Championship Living	343
	Exercise: Champions Don't Just Show Up for the Game	346
3	Tanny's Suggestion Checklist	347
4	Wrap-Up	355
	Exercise: Taking Stock	

Section 1

Personal Magic

Develop a "Magical Mind" (look within). Believe in magic. Now that you fully understand you are the <u>director, producer, star</u> in the unfolding story of your life. Taking personal responsibility is what it boils down to. Consult yourself – you have a higher invisible self that knows who you are, what you want, and <u>also </u>how to achieve it. Stop. Be still. Listen. Stop thinking the answers are "out there." Don't depend on others to tell you what you can and can't accomplish. Don't blame others for what you have not become! Stop making excuses.

You can and do choose the life you wish to lead. You have the power to turn your life into an ever-evolving masterpiece. The "secret," the key, lies within "your thoughts" – that invisible part of you, the "<u>higher you</u>." Leave behind old beliefs, old behaviors. Don't listen to, "You can't have, become, be...." Other people have overcome obstacles and conditions far worse than yours. The same force that allowed them to succeed is flowing through you, it's there for the taking. *Tap into it.*

Start believing you can do it.

As you look at each situation in life, you can be optimistic or pessimistic. You reflect and become in the physical world what you create in your invisible world.

Important: Start to picture in your head a picture of the kind of personality you wish to have (you already do this; however, you may not be aware of this), but have been imagining your self all along.

That is exactly how your personality got shaped.

Carpe Vitam   p. 341

You act upon those "inner visions" constantly. Once you know and accept that you chose the personality you possess, you can change what you don't like.

You can create the personality you wish to possess. Your physical behavior will start to reflect the new you. Self-talk is such a powerful tool – be aware of it.

Let go of doubt. You'll discover ways to carry out your purpose in life.

As Boethe said,

> *"Whatever you can do, or dream you can, begin it.*
> *Boldness has genius, power and <u>magic</u> in it.*
> *Begin it now."*

Section 2

Championship Living

Decide to Live a Championship Life

Champions have a coach (that's my job)

"Champions don't just show up for the game"

Champions are balanced beings – mentally – physically – spiritually.

> Become good at something. "Master it."
> Listen to yourself.
> Learn to trust yourself.

Like all champions, go to training camp. Champions see the big picture. Champions know the meaning of team spirit.

Physically go away if possible. If not, take private time to look at:

> Where you are;
>> Where you want to go;
>>> How you plan to get there.

A championship life is rewarding. "Go for the Gold."

To become a "**champion person**," the same rules apply as becoming a champion athlete. You will become good at what you do by practice, consciously and subconsciously practice your endeavor over and over until you witness an ease, a flow of grace in what you do. To people observing, it will look "easy," as if no effort is being expended.

Champions don't just show up for the game – they prepare.

Champions train. Champions go to a training camp.

Champions are balanced: emotionally, physically, socially, mentally, spiritually.

Carpe Vitam   p. 343

Champions believe in themselves.
Champions have made up their minds to be champions long before it happens.
Champions start acting like champs before it happens.
Champions acknowledge their success.
Champions enjoy their success.
Champions know that what they think about comes about.
Champions are not afraid of risk.
Champions understand the "thought" of winning attracts "the win."
Champions are confident in their abilities.
Champions never quit keeping in shape, never stop learning.
Champions have the *will* to win, the *will* to prepare.
Champions…are disciplined beings!

What do you wish to become a champion at?

Whatever you wish to become a champion at is within your reach!

Since we don't have referees in our lives, we tend to be sloppy. Become a referee, your own personal referee. Be disciplined. Be tough on yourself. Blow the whistle on your own poor behavior. Stop any behavior that is not propelling you toward your goals.

Everyone needs a cheering section. The world will not always give this to you. Become a cheerleader, your own personal cheerleader. Learn to tell yourself what a great job you have done. Acknowledge all of your wins. Stop seeking outside approval. Start rewarding yourself as you reach milestones.

Celebrate your victories, large and small. Reward yourself for completion of big jobs *and* small jobs.

Carpe Vitam   p. 344

Champions just don't show up for the game.

Start seeing yourself as a winner.

Example:

My son, Jonathan, was a middle distance runner in high school and <u>went to the Nationals</u>. His events were the 440 and the 880 yard run. Because of his running abilities, he was recruited by hundreds of colleges, including most of the Ivy League schools. He chose Stanford University and graduated four years later.

He kept winning race after race. I asked, "Jonathan, why do you think you keep winning?" He said, "I see myself going over the finish line first." In other words, he visualized winning. Jonathan was feeding his subconscious mind winning thoughts so clearly they became reality. In a relaxed state, your subconscious mind (dream state) does not know the difference between whether you are physically doing an activity or mentally doing it. <u>Your subconscious mind does not judge</u> – <u>it obeys its orders</u>. That is the reason I urged you earlier to feed your subconscious mind clear pictures of what you desire. Jonathan not only went out each day and ran 5 to 12 miles, he ran the race constantly <u>in his mind</u>. Awake and while sleeping.

Jonathan kept his body and mind in harmony and was willing to pay the price to be a superstar runner. He would get up at 6:00 a.m. on ice-cold, bitter mornings and go out and run. Jonathan was willing to do whatever it took to get the job done. This meant no junk food, no late-night parties, clean living. The choice was his. He accepted the challenge and did it. People came to watch him run. In some of his longer races, he would lap other runners, and there was a grace and beauty to his style. Jon made running look easy.

I, as his mom, can tell you, champions just don't show up for the game.

> **Long before they succeed and reach their goals,
> winners see themselves as winners.**

Carpe Vitam   p. 345

EXERCISE

Champions Don't Just Show Up for the Game

What do I plan to become a champion at?

_____
_____
_____
_____
_____
_____
_____
_____
_____
_____

What's my game plan?

_____
_____
_____
_____
_____
_____
_____
_____
_____
_____
_____
_____
_____
_____

Carpe Vitam   p. 346

Section 3

Tanny's Suggestion Checklist
(Things to consider/think about)

	YES	NO, NEEDS SOME WORK
Dare to dream.	❑	❑ _____
Don't buy somebody else's dream.	❑	❑ _____
Understand the greatest value in life is not what you get, it's what you become.	❑	❑ _____
Become all you were meant to be.	❑	❑ _____
Be willing to make mistakes.	❑	❑ _____
Be willing to risk.	❑	❑ _____
Become your own best friend.	❑	❑ _____
Don't get trapped into just making a living.	❑	❑ _____
Act – stop reacting.	❑	❑ _____
Be pro-active.	❑	❑ _____
Set goals.	❑	❑ _____
Invest in yourself.	❑	❑ _____
Trust yourself.	❑	❑ _____

Carpe Vitam   p. 347

	YES	NO, NEEDS SOME WORK
Be good to yourself.	❏	❏ _____
Develop a sense of humor.	❏	❏ _____
Don't take yourself so seriously.	❏	❏ _____
Don't join the easy crowd. Place yourself where the expectations are high.	❏	❏ _____
Don't ever stop learning.	❏	❏ _____
Don't compromise your values.	❏	❏ _____
Learn to ask the right questions (the good questions).	❏	❏ _____
Stay awake.	❏	❏ _____
Ask yourself, What's keeping you from living the life you want?	❏	❏ _____
Become an expert at something.	❏	❏ _____
Acknowledge the untapped talents you have.	❏	❏ _____
Let people know what you want.	❏	❏ _____
Expect to win.	❏	❏ _____
Know love/success is not in short supply.	❏	❏ _____
Know how to get what you want? Give people what they want.	❏	❏ _____

Carpe Vitam   p. 348

	YES	NO, NEEDS SOME WORK
Be around positive people.	❑	❑ _____
Play fair.	❑	❑ _____
Don't just be a taker, give.	❑	❑ _____
Always keep your word.	❑	❑ _____
Strive to be a balanced being.	❑	❑ _____
Be still.	❑	❑ _____
Be able to be alone (without being lonely).	❑	❑ _____
Enjoy today.	❑	❑ _____
Enjoy the little things.	❑	❑ _____
Be a possibility thinker.	❑	❑ _____
Understand your "purpose" in life.	❑	❑ _____
Smile.	❑	❑ _____
Choose success.	❑	❑ _____
Learn to receive, gracefully.	❑	❑ _____
Old beliefs no longer working must be "dumped."	❑	❑ _____
Keep physically active.	❑	❑ _____
Recognize self-imposed limitations (and get rid of them).	❑	❑ _____

Carpe Vitam p. 349

	YES	NO, NEEDS SOME WORK
Be flexible.	☐	☐ _____
Know problems will make you better or bitter. (Choose better.)	☐	☐ _____
Be involved in a cause bigger than yourself.	☐	☐ _____
Understand every problem brings an opportunity.	☐	☐ _____
Know success breeds success.	☐	☐ _____
Know success doesn't eliminate problems, it presents a new set.	☐	☐ _____
Your perception of a problem is more important than the problem.	☐	☐ _____
Know the past does not equal the future.	☐	☐ _____
Know the future is a potential.	☐	☐ _____
Know if you don't take control of your life, you give the control to someone else.	☐	☐ _____
When you can't solve a problem, "manage" it.	☐	☐ _____
Practice positive self-talk.	☐	☐ _____
Understand "What you think about comes about."	☐	☐ _____

Carpe Vitam   p. 350

	YES	NO, NEEDS SOME WORK
Know problems never leave you where you were, they propel you forward.	❑	❑ _____
Learn to turn your pain into profit.	❑	❑ _____
Ask what lessons you have learned from your setbacks.	❑	❑ _____
Try a new approach (if things aren't working).	❑	❑ _____
Don't count on others for emotional feedback; learn to give it to yourself.	❑	❑ _____
Be willing to learn to admit you don't know (but you'll find out).	❑	❑ _____
Have a plan.	❑	❑ _____
Know what you can live with/can't live with.	❑	❑ _____
Laugh.	❑	❑ _____
Learn to listen.	❑	❑ _____
Become fascinated, not frustrated.	❑	❑ _____
Let go, let the past die.	❑	❑ _____
Develop a network – personally, professionally.	❑	❑ _____
Pain in life is inevitable, suffering is optional.	❑	❑ _____

Carpe Vitam   p. 351

	YES	NO, NEEDS SOME WORK
Make good choices for yourself.	❏	❏ _____
Spend your energy wisely.	❏	❏ _____
Play.	❏	❏ _____
Be around children, older people.	❏	❏ _____
Mix it up (mundane chores).	❏	❏ _____
Take time out to relax.	❏	❏ _____
Help someone less fortunate.	❏	❏ _____
Understand people don't want you to change.	❏	❏ _____
Know what you want more of in your life.	❏	❏ _____
Know what you want less of in your life.	❏	❏ _____
Understand there is a price tag to anything of value.	❏	❏ _____
Count your blessings.	❏	❏ _____
Don't blame others for where you are in life.	❏	❏ _____
Learn to laugh at yourself.	❏	❏ _____
Always have an alternate plan.	❏	❏ _____
Never give up.	❏	❏ _____

Carpe Vitam

	YES	NO, NEEDS SOME WORK
Be self reliant.	❏	❏ _____
Know your emotions influence your health.	❏	❏ _____
Understand your success does not depend on anybody.	❏	❏ _____
Learn to deal with fear, it creates imaginary difficulties.	❏	❏ _____
Keep looking for the good opportunities.	❏	❏ _____
Don't be afraid to be wrong.	❏	❏ _____
Ask for help when you need it.	❏	❏ _____
When an opportunity presents itself – go for it.	❏	❏ _____
Stand for something.	❏	❏ _____
Stop sabotaging yourself.	❏	❏ _____
Learn to control your mental fears.	❏	❏ _____
Become a problem solver.	❏	❏ _____
Learn to interrupt negative behavior patterns.	❏	❏ _____
Be passionate about life.	❏	❏ _____
Be a true friend.	❏	❏ _____

Carpe Vitam   p. 353

	YES	NO, NEEDS SOME WORK
Daydream.	❑	❑ _____
Don't expect anyone to make you happy.	❑	❑ _____
Listen to your body, it tells you what it needs.	❑	❑ _____
Know what success is for you.	❑	❑ _____
Learn to look at the big picture.	❑	❑ _____
Simplify your life.	❑	❑ _____
Just because you think something is so – doesn't mean it's so – it's your perception.	❑	❑ _____
Be a resource for others. Be generous.	❑	❑ _____
There is no one right or wrong way to reach a solution.	❑	❑ _____
Understand everyone does not see the world as you see it.	❑	❑ _____
Build a history with people important to you.	❑	❑ _____
Know who you can always count on.	❑	❑ _____
Use the experts.	❑	❑ _____
Understand no one is perfect.	❑	❑ _____

Carpe Vitam   p. 354

Section 4

Wrap-Up
Taking Stock

It's time to do...

"The way my life looks right now."

Looking at each area of your life.

> What has changed?
>
> What did you learn?
>
> What did you feel good about?
>
> What did you feel sad about?
>
> What needs more work?
>
> What's working for you?
>
> What became clear to you?
>
> What do you plan to put more energy into?
>
> What would you like to explore more?
>
> What new insights do you have?
>
> What have I been neglecting?
>
> What do I want to spend more time on?

Once you've finished the exercise starting on the next page, I'd like you to compare it to the exact same exercise you did back in Chapter 1. I guarantee you'll see a lot of differences in your answers.

Carpe Vitam   p. 355

EXERCISE

Taking Stock
The way my life looks now

Date: _____
(If needed, use more paper)

Personally, right now I.....
_____
_____
_____
_____
_____
_____
_____

Career-Wise, right now I.....
_____
_____
_____
_____
_____
_____
_____

Financially, right now I.....
_____
_____
_____
_____
_____
_____
_____

Carpe Vitam   p. 356

Taking Stock

EXERCISE

Taking Stock
The way my life looks now

Date: _____
(If needed, use more paper)

Physically, right now I.....
_____
_____
_____
_____
_____
_____

Socially, right now I.....
_____
_____
_____
_____
_____
_____

Intellectually, right now I.....
_____
_____
_____
_____
_____
_____
_____

Taking Stock

Carpe Vitam   p. 357

EXERCISE

Taking Stock
The way my life looks now

Date: _____
(If needed, use more paper)

Emotionally, right now I.....
_____
_____
_____
_____
_____
_____

Spiritually, right now I.....
_____
_____
_____
_____
_____
_____

Relationships, right now I.....
_____
_____
_____
_____
_____
_____
_____

Taking Stock

Carpe Vitam   p. 358

Remember – Today is a gift.

That's why they call it "the present."

"Carpe Diem!"
(Seize the Day)

Carpe Vitam   p. 359

Chapter 9 Review Page - Carpe Vitam!

Carpe Vitam   p. 361

Carpe Vitam   p. 362

Final Words from Tanny

After being asked thousands of times, "What makes your life work?" I felt a need to write this book for you. What you need you already have – you. You're the obstacle you have been consciously or unconsciously using to keep you from reaching your goals of living the life you desire and deserve.

Please never forget that <u>you</u> are the director, producer, star in the unfolding story of your life. Taking personal responsibility is what it boils down to. Consult <u>yourself first</u>. In areas that you need help, consult the experts.

After reading and doing the exercises, answering the questions, writing your personal thoughts in this book, you now understand the answers are not "out there."

You have a higher, invisible self that knows who you are, what you want, and <u>also</u> how to achieve it.

You can and do choose the life you wish to lead. You have the power to turn your life into an ever-evolving masterpiece. The "secret" – the key – lies within "your thoughts" – that invisible part of you, the <u>higher</u> you.

Start tapping into it and use it for you. It will guide you to become what you want to become and live the life you once only dreamed of. Know and believe you deserve it.

You now know you must leave behind old beliefs and old behavior that are no longer working for you. Don't listen to "you can't" have, become, be. Other people have overcome obstacles and conditions far worse than yours. The same force that allowed them to succeed is flowing through you. It's there for the taking. Tap into it.

Please let me know how this workbook has helped you to live the life you desire. Write and tell me of your successes and which parts of the workbook were most helpful to you.

Start believing you can do it – I know you can!

I love my life and live it with enthusiasm, and I want the same for you. My sincere wish is that this book has shown you how to "Wake Up."

Disclaimer

The author makes no warranty of any kind with regard to this material, including, but not limited to, the implied warranties of merchantability, fitness for a particular pupose, or the owner's success in using or applying the suggestions contained herein or for incidental or consequential damages in connection with the furnishings, performance or use of this material.

This document contains proprietary information which is protected by copyright or trademark. All rights are reserved. NO PART of this document may be REPRODUCED, transmitted, transcribed, stored in a retrieval system, or translated into any language or computer language in any form or by any means, electronic, mechanical, magnetic, optical, chemical, manual or otherwise, WITHOUT the express written permission of **Sales Networks, Inc., P.O. Box 480, Cataumet, MA 02534, USA**.

If you would like information about seminars, keynotes, motivational speaking, business or personal lifestyle coaching, please call SNI at (508) 563-1988 or fax your request to (508) 563-7432.

Publisher's Note

This book is sold with the understanding that the publisher is not engaged in rendering psychological, financial, legal or other professional services. If assistance or counseling is needed, the services of a competent professional should be sought.

SNI is a trademark of Sales Networks, Inc.

Copyright ©1996 by Tanny McCarthy Mann

Who Is Tanny Mann?

Tanny Mann is the founder and President of Sales Networks, Inc., a company involved in business networking, now in its 14th year.

Since 1963, this veteran sales executive has launched four major industrial corporations and taught an astonishing number of commercially successful sales and marketing training seminars. Mann has been keynote speaker across the USA for many prestigious organizations and corporations.

Providing Business Coaching for entrepreneurial and start-up, as well as for large, well-established corporations, Tanny custom tailors the content of her presentations to address the issues most important to each audience. Her methods improve and help maintain individual performance, which, in turn, improves the entire organization. These techniques have proven especially effective in high-volume, high-pressure environments, and her "Refresher Talks" help to maintain cohesive, productive work groups as new staff members join the organization.

Her new book, "Life's Wake-Up Calls," is a result of the "Lifestyle Coaching" Tanny has been doing for individuals who wish to take responsibility for their future. People who have become *stuck,* both professionally and personally, have turned to Tanny for coaching. The workbook contains the information most used and asked for by her clients during the past 14 years.

Having been a long-time member of the New England Speakers Group (NESG), the National Speakers Association (NSA), the American Telemarketing Association, the International Women's Writing Guild, and a current member of the Writer's Guild of Cape Cod. Ms. Mann is an active speaker and trainer and has appeared on television and radio talk shows.

Practicing what she preaches and living her dream life on Cape Cod, Tanny believes the future is a potential - you design it. She gives you the tools needed to succeed. If you're not sure where you want to be professionally or personally and are ready to start pulling off your own miracles, call Tanny at (508) 563-1988.

Carpe Vitam   p. 365